Susan Sweet

BATTLEGROUND AMERICA

BURNSIDE'S BRIDGE

SO-AHC-635

BATTLEGROUND AMERICA

BURNSIDE'S BRIDGE
ANTIETAM

John Cannan

LEO COOPER

COMBINED PUBLISHING
Pennsylvania

COMBINED PUBLISHING

Copyright © 2001 John Cannan

ISBN 1-58097-035-4

For information, address:
COMBINED PUBLISHING
P.O. Box 307
Conshohocken, PA 19428
E-mail: combined@combinedpublishing.com
Web: www.combinedpublishing.com
Orders: 1-800-418-6065

Cataloging in Publication Data available from the Library of Congress.

Printed in the United States of America.

Published under license in Great Britain by

LEO COOPER
an imprint of
Pen & Sword Books Limited
47 Church Street, Barnsley, South Yorkshire S70 2AS

ISBN 0 85052 757 0

A CIP catalogue of this book is available
from the British Library

*For up-to-date information on other titles produced under the Leo Cooper imprint,
please telephone or write to:*
Pen & Sword Books Ltd, FREEPOST, 47 Church Street
Barnsley, South Yorkshire S70 2AS
Telephone 01226 734222

CONTENTS

To my wife, Christina Mary Borgeest

INTRODUCTION

THE LANDMARKS OF THE ANTIETAM NATIONAL BATTLEFIELD outside Sharpsburg, Maryland, sound deceptively pastoral devoid of their larger meaning. A map of the field almost seems a catalog of innocuously bucolic names: Burnside's Bridge, the West Wood, the Cornfield, the Dunker Church. Only one place, the Bloody Lane, connotes the murderous struggle that took place on 17 September 1862. Antietam's landmarks obtain their awful significance from the survivor's accounts of the fighting; the works of fine historians such as Carman, Sears, Murfin, and Priest; and the gruesome photographs taken of the fighting's aftermath. Yet studying the battle through these sources still cannot fully convey the experience of Civil War combat on the day when more Americans fell as casualties than in any battle before or since. We attempt to see in our mind's eye a described event, but our separation in distance and time hampers the effort. Scanning maps showing the unit positions and movements helps picture what happened, but these provide a coldly impersonal detachment from the fighting. Even photographs only show us a stationary fragment of the place as it existed around the time of the battle. Really, only by going to the battlefield itself and standing on the ground where the soldiers fought and died can one really come as close to the experiences of those who fought at the battle of Antietam. It is one thing to read about the heroic defense of the Georgians at Burnside's Bridge or the gallant charge of the *9th New York Zouaves* and another to see and pace over the terrain they struggled over.

The purpose of this book is to convey the experience of

one specific part of the battle of Antietam, the *IX Corps'* fateful struggle to take the Lower Bridge and assail the Confederate right flank. To accomplish this task, the main part of the book is a battle narrative. This is followed by a tour over the ground of the Antietam National Battlefield where this battle was fought, along with information about the field itself and other sources to learn more about the events that took place there and to plan a visit. This two-track approach is to provide a chronological narrative for the armchair traveler or the person wishing to study this part of the battle while also giving the battlefield visitor a guide to accompany a battlefield visit. Ideally, this book should be used in conjunction with other sources available in print and electronically as well as those provided by the National Park Service on the field itself. It is hoped that with these combined sources, a student of the battle will be able to go to the battlefield and better visualize the titanic struggle which ebbed and flowed over the farms and fields outside of Sharpsburg so many years ago.

CHAPTER 1

LEE'S 1862 INVASION OF MARYLAND

IN EARLY SEPTEMBER 1862, columns of troops waded through the placid waters of the Potomac River, then the border between the warring Northern and Southern states. These ranks were formed of ill-clad men, soldiers with a variety of different uniforms, many without even shoes, from nearly all the states that had seceded from the United States a year before to form the Southern Confederacy. Their numbers were leaving Virginian soil to invade the state of Maryland.

General Robert E. Lee boldly planned to campaign north of the Potomac River, telling President Davis on 3 September 1862, "The present seems to be the most propitious time since the commencement of the war for the Confederate Army to enter Maryland."

Lee would find to his discouragement that he would have to guard his campaign from loss soon after his army made its way into Maryland. On 4 September 1862, jubilant Confederate troops began to cross the icy waters of the Potomac River chanting the pro-Confederate anthem "Maryland, My Maryland." They headed north for Frederick, one of the state's largest cities, arriving on 6 September to find it decked out in banners and garlands to welcome the invading troops. While the reception may have been rousing, the substance behind the display's proved disappointing. Farmers and millers proved reluctant to offer the invading army the supplies it needed. The expected influx of manpower was also not forthcoming as Marylanders failed to flock to Lee's army in as large numbers as he had hoped. Worse still, his own ranks, already depleted from months of campaigning and fighting, were further reduced by rampant straggling. Some 10,000 troops may have left the army due to weariness, lack of shoes, or "unpatriotic feet." Others refused to join the army's march across the Potomac for the mere fact that they had enlisted to defend the South not invade the North.

Lee remained undaunted by the initial failure to achieve his campaign's objectives and resolved to stay north of the Potomac. His response was to undertake a bold gambit by moving westward across the South Mountain range to Hagerstown, 30 miles northwest from Frederick, which would become the base of a massive foraging expedition for his army. From there he would launch an incursion into central Pennsylvania's rich Cumberland Valley with a

Members of the Rebel army wade through the waters of the Potomac River during Lee's invasion of Maryland. (*Harper's Weekly*)

Robert E. Lee planned the bold move of the Army of Northern Virginia into Maryland in September 1862, which eventually led to the battle of Antietam.

more secure line of communications into Virginia laid farther west running through the Shenandoah Valley.

The only immediate obstacle Lee faced was a Federal garrison, 12,000 men strong, at Harper's Ferry, on the confluence of the Shenandoah and Potomac rivers, 25 miles west of Frederick. Initially, Lee had supposed his presence in Maryland would influence the force's evacuation. When this was not done, the Yankee troops became not only a danger that had to be remedied, but an opportunity to be realized. The opportunity was the abundance of Federal supplies that remained stockpiled in the town. Given Lee's disappointment over the scanty amount of goods supplied by loyal Marylanders and his army's need of shoes, clothes, and food, acquiring the material at Harper's Ferry became an attractive goal. Lee resolved that they should take the town before undertaking any grander movements into Pennsylvania.

To capture Harper's Ferry, Lee proposed dividing his army into several marching columns with troops. This required a temporary reorganization of his army. Before the movement, Jackson had four divisions in his corps while Longstreet had five. Lee jumbled these to create a large

Stonewall Jackson was given the task of taking the town of Harper's Ferry during the Southern foray into Maryland, which turned out to be an easy task due to the timid opposition he faced.

force for Jackson's Harper's Ferry operation composed of three divisions of his own corps along with three of Longstreet's divisions. These units were to accomplish seizure of the town by snaking through the countryside approaching Harper's Ferry from multiple directions, eventually surrounding the enemy force and sealing it from escape. Meanwhile, Longstreet with his remaining two divisions would march 20 miles northwest to Boonsboro where they would halt with the army's supply train. Jackson's remaining division under D. H. Hill would form the rearguard. Lee's choice of Jackson for the complicated Harper's Ferry operation was wise on its face. Jackson had won fame for performing spectacular tactical feats with his divisions on similar special missions.

Lee informed his commanders of his grand plan for the coming days with Special Orders 191 penned on 9 September. The plan was trademark Lee: bold and innovative, involving the division of his forces to accomplish several objectives. Nevertheless, this design was also dangerously reckless. If a substantial Union force appeared to face the Army of Northern Virginia with all its forces divided and north of the Potomac, it might be able to defeat the smaller contingents in detail. Lee was confident that his opponents would not have such a force massed against him until Harper's Ferry was taken and his army was reunited. On the day Special Orders 191 were issued, the Army of Northern Virginia went into motion, preparing to draw the net that would capture the Harper's Ferry garrison. Jackson's command separated into its separate columns that approached the town from the north, south, and west. On 12 and 13 September, Confederate troops were taking positions overlooking the town.

Jackson invested Harper's Ferry without too much difficulty. The town, surrounded by looming heights on all sides, was extremely difficult to defend even by the thousands of Union troops encamped there. To make matters worse for the imperiled Federal garrison, their leader, Colonel Dixon Miles, conducted an uninspired and timid opposition against the Confederate forces. Only one severe battle took place between the garrison and Jackson's men. This was on Maryland Heights with the Northerner's withdrawing from their critical position there after someone called a retreat. With Miles's Federals sent scurrying for safety in the town, Jackson's Confederates were easily able to seal the garrison's fate.

Following the Maryland Heights fight, the Confederates hauled cannons up the steep slopes overlooking Harper's Ferry and opened a frightening bombardment of the town on 14 September. The next day, Miles capitulated and Jackson's victorious Confederates entered the town. Miles was spared what probably would have been a humiliating investigation of his command at Harper's Ferry when he was struck and mortally wounded by a shell fired mistakenly after a truce had been made.

Despite this easy victory, Lee continued to have his ambitions in Maryland thwarted. Union forces were on the march against him much quicker than he anticipated. Even as Jackson was falling on Harper's Ferry, a reorganized *Army of the Potomac* was advancing west from Washington and preparing to fall upon Lee's divided forces, threatening to crush them while they were still vulnerably separated over miles of Maryland countryside.

CHAPTER 2

THE BATTLE OF ANTIETAM

PRUDENCE, perhaps, dictated that Lee should have abandoned the Maryland campaign after the relative success of his 14 September delaying action at South Mountain and the surrender of Harper's Ferry the next day. Nevertheless the Confederate commander was ill-disposed to abandon his efforts at invasion just yet and retreat to the relative safety of northern Virginia. Instead, though briefly considering a retreat across the Potomac, he decided to have his army fall back only as far as Sharpsburg, a sleepy Maryland crossroads town. On the evening of 14 September and the early morning of 15 September, his troops made the march from their battered defenses on South Mountain through Middletown and went into position on the farms and fields of Sharpsburg, an almost 17-mile trek marked by the litter of an army on the retreat.

The choice of Sharpsburg was an excellent one, granting the Confederate general many advantages and opportunities in the coming struggle. Whether Lee chose to mass his army in defiance of General George McClellan and his *Army of the Potomac* or avoid another contest by retreating, both options could easily be undertaken at Sharpsburg. From that town, a road extended to Jackson's location at Harper's Ferry, enabling the divisions there an easy path to rejoin the rest of the army. West of town, a road led to Boteler's Ford at the Potomac from whence Lee's troops could head into Virginia if Lee's army had to escape from Maryland.

Another factor in Lee's decision was the advantages the ground provided for making a stand against an aggressive

A view of the Lower (Burnside's) Bridge at the time of the Civil War (above) and today (below.)

Army of the Potomac. The terrain around the town was naturally well-suited for a defense, with rises, trees, limestone outcroppings and farmers' stone, and wooden rail fences providing protection and precluding the need to wear troops out building extensive trenches or breastworks. The Antietam Creek ran east of the town heading south from Pennsylvania, a potential hindrance to any Union assault. Only three bridges traversed its waters before the town with a fourth farther south at the stream's confluence with the Potomac.

Even with such fine defensible ground, taking a position at Sharpsburg was also a gamble. Of vital concern to the Confederate army was the Potomac River snaking its way east only three miles west of the town. The danger that waterway posed was palpable. If Lee had to retreat quickly for Boteler's Ford, crossing the Potomac there would be extremely difficult with an enemy close on the rear of his fleeing column. If his command were broken in battle, it could even be driven into the river's waters and destroyed.

Lee was confident he would neither be driven into the river nor be forced to retreat and prepared to make a stand. It was a decision that seems almost alternately courageous, brazen, and foolhardy. On 15 September, Lee had few troops with him to defend his position with only 15,000 men on hand to fend off the much larger *Army of the Potomac.* These men Lee set up in a segmented defensive belt before Sharpsburg, taking advantage of the area's many natural defenses and concealments. Of the Antietam's crossings, Lee only chose one point to dispute, the bridge immediately southeast of Sharpsburg, called the Rohrbach Bridge (after the nearby farm of Henry Rohrbach) or the Lower Bridge—it was soon to be known ever afterward as Burnside's Bridge.

Fortunately for Lee, McClellan was not disposed to rush to a confrontation at Sharpsburg. When dawn on 15 September uncovered the Confederate move from South Mountain, the *Army of the Potomac* traced Lee's path to the town. Once outside Sharpsburg, rather than engage the enemy immediately, McClellan decided to bide his time. Feeling it was too late in the day to launch an immediate attack, he went about concentrating and organizing his forces. But his activities took a substantial length of time and had the effect of strengthening the enemy.

After the 15th passed without major confrontation, Stonewall Jackson was allowed to arrive on the 16th with three of his divisions, effectively doubling the strength of Lee's Sharpsburg lines. Three more divisions were still away from the field. Two, part of Longstreet's Corps, were on the march from Harper's Ferry. The final one, Major General A. P. Hill's division of Jackson's Corps, remained in the town, paroling thousands of Yankee prisoners and disposing of the huge stocks of supplies and equipment that the Confederates had captured there.

The Confederate position at Sharpsburg had Jackson's Corps holding the left flank of Lee's line, most of his divisions grouped together north of Sharpsburg, many of his troops concealed in the West Woods, just off the Hagerstown Turnpike, and in a large 30-acre cornfield belonging

Union General George McClellan's caution allowed the Southern army to double its strength on the banks of the Antietam in the town of Sharpsburg. (National Archives)

to David R. Miller. Longstreet's divisions were more spread-out in a long line running above, before, and below the town. D. H. Hill's division, battle-weary from its efforts at South Mountain, lay in a sunken farm lane northeast of town connecting the Hagerstown and Boonsboro Turnpikes. Two more of Longstreet's divisions, D. R. Jones's and John Walker's, held a position roughly paralleling the Harper's Ferry Road behind the Lower Bridge. Longstreet's two other divisions were kept near Lee's headquarters west of Sharpsburg when they arrived from Harper's Ferry during the night. Even though Lee's numbers at Sharpsburg were increasing as McClellan waited, the *Army of the Potomac* still greatly outnumbered the Confederates. McClellan had five corps of more than 70,000 men, twice the number his opponent could field, with thousands of reserves nearby. Yet still he bided his time for no particular advantage or effect.

As 16 September passed into oblivion, McClellan proved daunted by the strength of the enemy position and again failed to display an aggressive temperament, choosing to inspect the ground for what he correctly perceived would be "a terrible battle." There was some cannonading and skirmishing throughout the day, but an engagement of any real significance was postponed for the future. The playing out of the coming confrontation was being pieced together in McClellan's mind.

The plan McClellan eventually designed for battle was deceptively simple: hit the Confederates hard on their left flank with the *I, II,* and *XII Corps* and on the right flank with the *IX Corps* in the hopes that the combined pressure would eventually splinter the thin enemy line. Still, even this simplistic design suffered from some complexity, the major problem being the prominence of each corps' role in the fight, especially the *IX Corps'* part.

To meet McClellan's goals, elements of the *Army of the Potomac* stirred into activity on 16 September. The *I Corps* moved at 1400 to cross the Antietam taking position north of Jackson's position at Sharpsburg. The *XII Corps* followed later in the evening finding its jump off point for the next day northeast of Hooker. Still east of the Antietam was Sumner's *II Corps* ranks and Porter's *V Corps*, located near the Middle Bridge with the *Army of the Potomac*'s cavalry division acting as the reserve. Finally, the *IX Corps* was positioned east of the Lower Bridge, marking the southern most point of the army. By Wednesday, 17 September, McClellan was ready to launch a gambit to vanquish the Army of Northern Virginia once and for all.

While the idea behind McClellan's plan was sound—simultaneous thrusts at either enemy flank—difficulties arose in the execution. The *Army of the Potomac*'s several corps, in powerful columns of thousands of men, hammered the Confederates' line like a mailed fist throughout the day, each having the potential to break their opposition. But the blows that were struck were uncoordinated, landing at different times and seldom in concert with the progress another had made. Since each of these attacks took place separately from one another, Lee could parry each by shifting his inferior forces to those places that were under the greatest strain. However, the Confederate general had a limited number of troops and their ability to maintain the fight was exhaustible. The Army of Northern Virginia's ability to withstand continued attacks began to falter as its casualties mounted into the thousands.

As the battle of Antietam unfolded, much of the major activity in the morning occurred to the north and northeast of Sharpsburg. The first of McClellan's blows was executed by Major General Joseph "Fighting Joe" Hooker, who began the Federal onslaught around 0600 driving on Sharpsburg from the north with 8,600 men. His troops tangled with brigades from Stonewall Jackson's Corps, totaling almost 1,000 men less than the *I Corps'* numbers, in a series of bloody charges and countercharges near a small whitewashed structure on the Hagerstown Turnpike—the Dunker Church—and the Miller cornfield, afterwards called "The Cornfield." It was a murderous fight. Hooker later wrote that Confederates slaughtered by Federal fire in

Major General Joseph Hooker led the first Union assault at Sharpsburg in "The Cornfield" of Antietam legend. He would later say he considered the battle there to be the most bloody and dismal he ever witnessed.

The Cornfield lay in rows, mimicking the ranks they had held before being cut down: "It was never my fortune to witness a more bloody, dismal battlefield." A soldier in the *6th Wisconsin* remembered of the cannon fire his unit was subjected to while on the charge: "We had marched ten rods when whizz! Bang! Burst a shell over our heads; then another; then a percussion shell struck and exploded in the very center of the moving mass of men. It killed two and wounded eleven. It tore off Captain David K. Noyes' foot and cut off both arms of a man in his company." The conflagration between the *I Corps* and Jackson finally ground to a halt before 0730 in a bloody stalemate. Whole commands had been chewed up in the grisly maw of death. The *I Corps* lost nearly 2,500 men in the action, almost a third of its numbers. Confederate forces had suffered severely as well. When Brigadier General John Bell Hood was later asked about his division, he responded that it was "dead on the field." John R. Jones's force, Jackson's old division, lost 33 percent of its soldiers killed or wounded, while Brigadier General Alexander Lawton's division saw

Confederate General John Bell lost most of his division in the terrible battle in The Cornfield at Antietam.

its strength cut in half. The losses were just as palpable at the regimental level. The 4th and 5th Texas and 18th Georgia were at half strength from the fighting. The 1st Texas was completely decimated, losing 186 out of 226 men brought into the contest, 82 percent of its strength. And this was only the first phase of the battle.

The next strikes wielded by the *Army of the Potomac* saw their impact denuded by battlefield confusion. As Major General Joseph Mansfield's 7,200-strong *XII Corps* entered the fray, Mansfield led them with the words, "Ah, boys. We shall do a fine thing today. We have got them where we want them. They cannot escape by the skin of their teeth." This infusion of fresh troops went mostly for naught. The *XII Corps* only lent ineffectual assistance after Mansfield was mortally wounded while trying to sort out if soldiers in front of his ranks were friend or foe.

Much of the corps remained stalled just east of where Hooker had been engaged though one division, George S.

Greene's, did manage to get a toehold in the Confederate line. It tapped the flank of the enemy's position, driving them back into the West Woods, and reached the plateau near the Dunker Church where it held on in the face of enemy fire. A member of the *111th Pennsylvania* remembered of the combat there:

> Without nervousness or haste the men monotonously loaded and discharged their pieces, and officers walked back and forth shouting orders . . . Every moment men went down, some with wounds so slight they were unheeded, some disabled for life, and some to rise no more. Throats were parched from thirst. Faces were blackened with smoke, lips smeared and cracked with powder from bitten cartridges. The guns were so hot that their brass bans were discolored. Belts sagged loosely over empty stomachs. Hands were swollen with the incessant use of the ramrod. Shoulders were lamed by the recoil of pieces.

Despite Greene's advantageous position, he never received any support to exploit its success and was forced to pull back.

General Joseph Mansfield was mortally wounded while leading the *XII Corps* during the battle of Antietam. He had only taken command of the corps two days before. (National Archives)

When the *II Corps* had been called to the battle around 0720, the stage was set for the action to shift to another part of the field. One sad act remained to be played before this could occur. Boasting 15,400 men, the *II Corps* should have laid the decisive blow to smash Jackson's battered division. Instead the force suffered one of the greatest tragedies experienced by a Union command that day. This occurred when Major General John Sedgwick's 5,400-man division managed to get separated from the corps' two other divisions as it advanced in a tight formation of three compact parallel lines about 60 to 70 yards apart into the West Woods. Once among the trees, the command found itself in a pocket of enemy fire from the front, left flank, and rear. As luck would have it, Confederate reinforcements, through no design or coordination, were converging on Sedgwick's unsuspecting left flank. The Federals could not have stumbled into a better trap if the Rebels had planned it. Corps commander Edwin Sumner only realized the peril to Sedgwick's men when an officer shouted, "See! The Rebels!"

A depiction of the battle in the West Woods where 2,100 men in Sedgwick's division were lost in less than 15 minutes. (*Harper's Weekly*)

General John Sedgwick's division met a deadly fate in the West Woods around Sharpsburg after they became seperated from the rest of the *II Corps* and found themselves surrounded on three sides by Confederate troops. (Library of Congress)

"My God!" exclaimed Sumner. "We must get out of this." Before the general's troops could react, an explosion of musketry erupted on their left flank cutting down men in the front and rear. Confusion and hysteria swept through the ranks, the combat's deafening din forcing officers to resort to hand gestures to communicate commands when their voices could not be heard over the fire. Some commanders and men tried to hold their ground and returned fire, others stampeded for safety. Under so terrible a fire, it quickly became obvious that Sedgwick's embattled position in the West Woods was untenable. A retreat was called with the survivors of the battle streaming north for safety. In nearly 15 minutes, 2,100 men had become casualties, many before being able to fire a shot in reply. Most of the Confederate force involved in the destruction of Sedgwick's division—John G. Walker's Division and George T. Anderson's Brigade—had been detached from the Confederate right flank that had remained unengaged throughout most of the morning.

The two other divisions of the *II Corps* enjoyed more success against the center of the Army of Northern Virginia's line though at a heavy cost. The division that was supposed to support Sedgwick's command had veered south-east during its advance to a ridge before a sunken road held by brigades from Major General D. H. Hill of Jackson's Division. A destructive fusillade belched forth from the Confederate lines, staggering French's division as it came on. A ferocious firefight with Hill's men quickly followed with men falling dead and wounded by the scores. Still, the Confederate position was a strong one and the troops in the road held up against blasting fusillades. French's division took a heavy toll for their attack, 1,750 men as casualties, nearly a third of the force.

Reinforcements for French were on the way in the form of the *II Corps'* final division, the *1st* under Major General Israel Richardson. The addition of these troops and the mounting stacks of casualties and confusion in the sunken road enabled the Federals to drive into the Confederate position there and scatter the brigades that had so desperately opposed them. It was about noon when the Federals finally took the position. As an indication of how intense the fire had been, Colonel John B. Gordon had been hit five times while directing his troops. The final bullet caused the officer to fall face forward into his hat. Had the head piece

The commander of the *II Corps*, General Edwin Sumner, realized too late the deadly fate Sedgwick's division faced.

not been pierced by a bullet, the colonel might have met a gruesome death, drowning in the blood flowing forth from a neck wound. One Yankee of the *5th New Hampshire* recalled of the lane's carnage: "In this road lay so many dead rebels that they formed a line which one might have walked upon as far as I could see, many of whom had been killed by the most horrible wounds of shot and shell, and they just lay there as they had been killed apparently, amid the blood which was soaking the earth." With the demise of Confederate resistance in the Sunken Road, or by its more apt name, Bloody Lane, the center of Lee's line had cracked open.

Richardson's advance continued over the fields between the road and Sharpsburg. But so close to victory, a barrage of Confederate artillery threw the division of Northerners back. Israel Richardson combed the field for troops and batteries to renew the success his command had thus far enjoyed. A shell fragment deprived the Federal cause of this drive and energy striking the officer just as he paused to take a drink of water. The injured Richardson was carried from the field. With Richardson's fall passed the chance that the Federals might renew their offensive west of the Sunken Road.

Richardson's work and that of so many others need not have been in vain. McClellan had plenty of men to throw behind further attacks north and east of Sharpsburg. The 6,600-man *V Corps* had seen little action thus far on its reserve duty. Franklin's *VI Corps* was also on hand after it had come to the battlefield around 0900 bringing a further 10,000 men. These vast ranks would go unused. McClellan would not chance using his reserves for fear doing so would leave him vulnerable to the superior numbers he supposed Lee to have. One of McClellan's subordinates who had survived the day's fighting was also drained of fervor. General Sumner, after the debacle in the West Woods, dissuaded McClellan from allowing a pugnacious Franklin to throw his troops into the action—the initiative was in the hands of the *Army of the Potomac*, won at the

General Daniel H. Hill

General William H. French

General Israel B. Richardson

General John B. Gordon

expense of thousands of men killed, injured, and wounded, yet its commanders did not have the resolve to use it.

The Southern lack of a significant manpower reserve was more of a problem on the other side of the field. The *Army of the Potomac*'s continued attacks, while not effective in crushing the Confederate line, were taking their toll through attrition. Though the soldiers of the Army of Northern Virginia demonstrated a dedicated unyielding tenacity to withstand the overwhelming pressure being applied against them, casualties had severely depleted their ranks and more units had been completely decimated by the day's engagements. Confederate officers scoured the field for survivors of shattered commands, gathering them up to stave off future enemy attacks. Only a flimsy line maintained the Confederate center against any renewed Union assault there. A noon dispatch from Lee's headquarters to General William Pendleton, near Shephardstown, reflected his desperation: "If you have fifteen or twenty guns, suitable for our purpose, which you can spare, the general desires you to send them with a sufficiency of ammunition. You must not take them from the fords if essential to their safety. Send up the stragglers. Take any cavalry about there and send up at the point of the sword. We want ammunition, guns, and provisions." Pendleton was not able to send much aid. The only force that Lee could count on to provide a fresh influx of manpower was A. P. Hill's division on the march from Harper's Ferry.

With the initiative sacrificed on this part of the field, the last chance for a significant Federal victory fell on the final major assault to be made that day, that by Major General Ambrose Burnside's *IX Corps* against the far Confederate right flank held by Brigadier General David R. Jones on the southeastern vicinity of Sharpsburg.

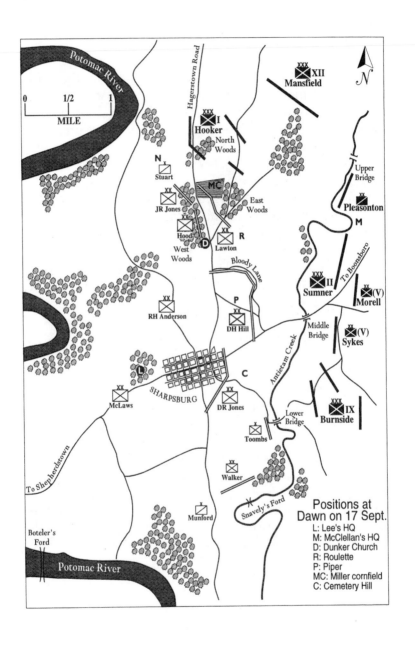

Positions at
Dawn on 17 Sept.

L: Lee's HQ
M: McClellan's HQ
D: Dunker Church
R: Roulette
P: Piper
MC: Miller cornfield
C: Cemetery Hill

CHAPTER 3

FACE OFF AT BURNSIDE'S BRIDGE

ON A FIELD FRAUGHT with agony and bloodshed, lost hopes and might-have-beens, the fighting at Burnside's Bridge was as fitting a culmination to the drama as any veteran author of fiction could have penned. The soldiers' numbers and the tally of casualties were fewer than those involved in the mighty struggles for the West Woods and The Cornfield. Yet it was around Burnside's Bridge that McClellan's hopes for victory would come closest to being realized and where one of the most amazing tenacious defenses would be fought by Lee's men.

On the morning of 17 September 1862 the flanks of the two contending armies were engaged in a standoff, separated by a rolling landscape overlain with the trappings of farm life. Two major roads, the Boonsboro Pike and the Harper's Ferry Road, along with the narrow valley of the Antietam Creek roughly defined the area of action around Burnside's Bridge, hereinafter referred to as the Lower Bridge. The Boonsboro Pike defined the northernmost extent of the action, a route extending east from Sharpsburg, crossing the Antietam Creek at the Middle Bridge. Forming the western border of the fighting was the Harper's Ferry Road, leading almost directly south from the town along the high ground and slowly inclining its way to the southeast. The path of the Antietam valley below the Middle Bridge formed the contest's winding eastern and southern borders. From the Middle Bridge, the creek made a circuitous route south, flowing almost directly southeast before sweeping southwest just above the Lower Bridge.

A present-day photo of Burnside's Bridge.

Below that span, the Antietam meandered sharply, carving out an "s" in the earth, before again continuing its southeasterly course. Again, the creek curved sharply to the west as it approached its confluence with the Potomac River.

Like the ground both the *Army of the Potomac* and the Army of Northern Virginia had fought over to the north, the earth between these landmarks was also rippled in undulations of ridges and hills severed by deep depressions, but with some ascents and descents deeper and steeper than those found north and east of Sharpsburg. The highest ground was a rolling ridge running southwest to northeast on a path that took it across the Harper's Ferry Road and up to Sharpsburg's eastern face. East of this prominence, the ground sloped away downward toward the Antietam through intervening elevations, cleaved by two ravines. The southernmost of these followed the course of a wash that began just east of the Harper's Ferry Road, nearly 2,000 feet from the town, bending the level of the high ground there as it cut slightly southeast through the slope. Nearly 2,000 feet along its path, a broad ravine cradled the wash as it made a more direct southerly course, extending all the way to the Antietam, with branches extending east and west where it closed in on the stream. Another ravine, holding a spring branch, extended from southeastern Sharpsburg, widening as it went, running east the full extent of the distance between the town and the creek. Both ravines nearly intersected, almost making a rough "T," but remained separated by a band of less depressed ground. Near the course of the Antietam, the land rose to form a chain of hills before falling sharply into the bluffs that made up the western edge of the stream's valley. East of these, the stream flowed on the valley floor that began a slow ascent before rising again into low heights on the eastern side of its bank. Across from the Lower Bridge were two small hills, both around 110 feet in height, their eastern faces made up of gradually increasing steepness. One was almost directly across from the bridge itself, slightly to the northeast, while the other was some 300 yards to the southeast. Beyond a ravine, east and slight-

A present-day view looking over the ground where Maxcy Gregg's and L. O'Brian Branch's brigades were engaged on the Otto Farm.

ly south of the second hill, the ground rose to even greater heights.

As was the case around Sharpsburg, the land here too had been divided into a patchwork of tilled agricultural fields, some plowed, others carpeted with stubble or pasture ground, still others contained small orchards or were filled with stalks of corn. Most were bordered by long fences, many composed of wooden rails, some of stone. Two of the more prominent local farms were found on this ground, the southernmost one, belonging to John Otto and the other to Joseph Sherrick.

Besides the Harper's Ferry Road and the Boonsboro Pike, a few other routes traversed the area. One was a road that emerged from the very southeastern edge of Sharpsburg, alternately named after the sites it passed on its path: the Lower Bridge Road, the Rohrbach Bridge Road, or the Rohrsville Road. Heading on a gently bending diagonal path southeast from Sharpsburg, it descended through the ravine there that led toward the Antietam Creek, paralleling the spring branch. Around 600 yards from the town it passed north of the Otto House and south of the Sherrick home. Roughly 1,000 yards from the town, the road turned

A present-day photo with the Sherrick House on the left and behind the trees on the right the white Otto House. The road that ran between the two houses during the Civil War led to the Lower Bridge over the Antietam Creek.

A view looking south down the Lower Bridge Road from the eastern mouth of Burnside's Bridge.

south to follow the Antietam for 400 yards before it abruptly turned east to cross the stream at the Lower Bridge. Once on the eastern bank, the road veered almost directly south again, tracing again the Antietam's course more than 300 yards past the lands of the Henry Rohrbach Farm. Then it departed from the waterway heading on a southeasterly and then easterly direction that would eventually take it to the town of Rohrsville.

Besides the Lower Bridge Road, a few farmers' lanes also had been carved out on the soil. On ground east of the Lower Bridge, a farm lane ran from the Lower Bridge Road, 250 yards south of the span north over the eastern bluffs to the Rohrbach Farm, running through a ravine between the two hills east of the bridge. Shortly below this, another lane veered away from the Lower Bridge heading northeastward to Porterstown. West of the stream, a path emanated from the Otto Farm heading directly south making one pronounced zigzag along the way. Otto's neighbor Sherrick also had a farm lane, heading directly north to connect with the Boonsboro Pike.

Over this landscape of hills and ravines, fields, fences, and farm lanes, lay the Confederate far right flank, a position that had become of increasing importance as the day progressed. Here, by the waning morning hours of 17 September 1862, the Army of Northern Virginia's fate was in the hands of Brigadier General David Rumph Jones, one of Robert E. Lee's more obscure but experienced division commanders. West Point graduate Jones, curiously nicknamed "Neighbor," like many Civil War officers on both sides had tasted warfare in the 1846-1848 conflict with Mexico in which he had won brevets for good service.

General David R. "Neighbor" Jones led the Confederate division charged with the defense of the Lower Bridge. His force was sizably smaller than the Union force it faced. (Library of the University of North Carolina)

On the Antietam battlefield, Jones would meet one of the sorest tests a soldier could face. His five brigades, complemented only by a handful of artillery batteries and some horsemen, were charged with holding an elongated defensive position against an enemy more than four times his strength in manpower. It seemed an impossible task given the odds and it made for one of the most dramatic moments of the Civil War.

Jones's division indeed had a wide front to cover: a one-and-a-half-mile line laid out on the high ground immediately east and south of Sharpsburg, his ranks stretching from the Boonsboro Pike around the town to the Harper's Ferry Road. G. T. Anderson's Brigade had held the left of the line on the Boonsboro Pike earlier in the day but was ordered north around 0730, when the line's left became the responsibility of Pickett's Brigade of Virginia regiments. Under Brigadier General Richard B. Garnett, it was spread out, east of Sharpsburg, between Boonsboro Pike and the road leading to the Lower Bridge. Extending the line farther south was Jenkins's Brigade of South Carolinians under Colonel Joseph Walker in position south of Lower Bridge Road in front of Sharpsburg's southeastern corner. Brigadier General Thomas F. Drayton's brigade was next with his command of Georgians and South Carolinians, followed by Brigadier General James L. Kemper's brigade made up entirely of regiments from Virginia. Strategically placed throughout this position was an assortment of artillery posted on a prominence just outside Sharpsburg and south of the Boonsboro Pike. Since this elevation was near a graveyard, it came to be called Cemetery Hill in the battle reports and reminiscences.

Situated on the high ground outside Sharpsburg, Jones's men had a good view of the terrain before them as it sloped up and down toward the narrow valley of the Antietam. More important, Jones's artillery enjoyed a clear line of sight nearly all the way to the bridge. For a battle that would become known as "Artillery Hell," the broad view the Confederate gunners enjoyed south of Sharpsburg meant they would play a major role in the fighting to come.

Jones would need all the advantages he could possibly obtain since his infantry strength was pathetically weak. Several Southern commanders and troops who wrote about Sharpsburg are almost apologetic in their description of the numbers mustered to fight in Jones's line. Months of heavy fighting and the long marches from Richmond to Northern Virginia and Maryland had taken a huge toll on the strength of Lee's army and were especially telling in Jones's Division. Brigades numbered a few hundred men at most, some regiments could not even field a hundred soldiers, and several companies consisted of only a handful of troops. Overall, Jones's Division counted only as many as 3,000 men total. Fortunately for Jones, the geography before him provided an ideal opportunity to use a modest number of troops to effectively contest the enemy's advance.

Since the Lower Bridge was the only crossing of the Antietam that the Army of Northern Virginia would contest during the battle, Jones had a considerable portion of his force, some 400 men of the 2nd and 20th Georgia regiments, move into position on the bluffs overlooking the span, nearly 1,200 yards before his main line. The 20th Georgia, under Colonel John B. Cumming, was on the line's left, extending some 40 yards to the north of the bridge. A handful of men from this regiment were in a most advantageous post in a quarry close to the top of the bluff. Overlooking the western mouth of the bridge provided a point from which the troops could fire down the length of the span. Lieutenant Colonel William R. Holmes's 2nd Georgia occupied the right flank of the bridge line, extending far enough to overlook the creek's bend eastward and where the Lower Bridge Road began to run alongside the creek.

A present day photo of Burnside's Bridge taken from the area of the Georgian entrenchments.

General Robert A. Toombs led some of the Confederate units defending the Lower Bridge. (National Archives)

Besides the Rebel troops overlooking the bridge, a collection of infantry and cavalry guarded Antietam's fording points farther south. A few hundred more men were on the right flank of the 2nd and 20th Georgia. They belonged to Lieutenant Colonel Frank Kearse's 50th Georgia detached from Drayton's Brigade, and a company from Jenkin's Brigade, along with some companies from the 11th Georgia left behind by G. T. Anderson. A cavalry force was even farther south. They were to obstruct the enemy attempts to ford the Antietam south of the Lower Bridge and then to fall back to the right of the main line when this goal no longer became possible.

The Confederate forces at the bridge could also count on artillery support though the location of the guns turned out to be problematic. A light field battery, Captain J. B. Richardson's 2nd Company of the Washington Artillery, was on hand 500 yards to the west, but they were believed to be too far away to help the infantry at the bridge and General Longstreet was prevailed upon for some more cannon. "Old Pete" responded by sending Captain J. L. Eubank's battery of Colonel S. D. Lee's artillery battalion which took up position between the Antietam and Richard-son's guns.

This collection of forces before the bridge was headed by a dual command structure with Brigadier General Robert Augustus Toombs commanding all the units there and Colonel Henry L. Benning immediately in charge of the 2nd and 20th Georgia regiments. Neither Confederate commander here had much prewar military experience.

Toombs's and Benning's advance force and the brigades outside Sharpsburg were all the forces Jones had on hand to make his defense. While he detached troops to the fighting on the left, it was unlikely that any of his comrades would be extending him a similar favor. Parrying Union thrusts of several corps had exhausted and bloodied the rest of the Army of Northern Virginia on the field. Now there was no reserve available to reinforce those areas in need of help. Jones could only expect assistance from A. P. Hill's division, on the road from Harper's Ferry, and even that might not be enough to counter the Federal ranks arrayed against him.

To realize the palpable threat Jones faced, one need only tally the Federal strength he opposed. A considerable Union force was preparing to go into action against the Confederate right on 17 September. The *IX Corps* was 12,500-men strong in four divisions: the *1st* under Brigadier General Orlando B. Willcox, the *2nd* under Brigadier General Samuel D. Sturgis, the *3rd* under Brigadier General Isaac P. Rodman, and *Kanawha Division* under Colonel Eliakim P. Scammon. Their commander was the bewhiskered Major General Ambrose E. Burnside.

If numbers alone could decide the course of a battle, the *IX Corps* units should have easily brushed aside the numerically smaller Confederate force that opposed it. Several factors, however, worked to offset the formidable power of the larger Yankee battalions. One was the eruption of a petty tiff between Generals McClellan and Burnside. Events during the Maryland Campaign placed a heavy strain on their friendship, causing its warmth to cool into

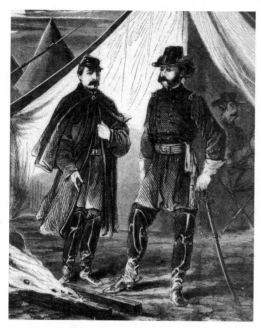

A petty tiff between Generals McClellan (left) and Burnside (right) threatened the Union chain of command at the battle of Antietam.

mere tepidness. McClellan had criticized Burnside for what he thought was a sluggish pursuit of the Confederates after South Mountain and remonstrated with Burnside in a curt dispatch demanding an explanation for his tardiness. McClellan compounded this reproach with another on 16 September, claiming Burnside had been slow getting his troops into position on the field outside Sharpsburg.

Burnside, for his part, was bitterly dissatisfied with the reorganization the *Army of the Potomac* had taken after South Mountain. Before that battle, Burnside was a wing commander in control of two corps, his own and Major General Joseph Hooker's *I Corps*. Now at Sharpsburg, McClellan had dispensed with the wing command structure without really informing his commanders. When McClellan dispatched the *I Corps* to the opposite flank of the Federal line at Sharpsburg, far away from Burnside's command, the *IX Corps* commander regarded the move as an embarrassing demotion and affront. A wing commander without a wing, Burnside still sulkily acted as though he

Orlando Willcox was the new leader of the Union *1st Division, IX Corps*, at the battle of Antietam, a post he had taken after the death of General Isaac Stevens. (USAMHI)

maintained the position anyway and kept another commander in control of the *IX Corps,* Brigadier General Jacob Cox.

Cox was understandably nervous about assuming such great responsibility in the face of a major battle. He did not have the staff on hand to undertake such a task easily and he was new to this theater of action. Upon learning that McClellan had detached Hooker and his *I Corps* from Burnside's "wing," Cox begged his superior to retake corps command. Burnside politely refused the request, arguing he was still in charge of a formation of several corps.

The situation was not only awkward for Cox; it created an unnecessarily complex network of communication between the *Army of the Potomac*'s headquarters and those of the *IX Corps*. When McClellan dispatched his orders, Burnside would pass them on to Cox to implement them with the assistance of Burnside's staff. Making matters worse, the potential of both Burnside and Cox to command was seriously impaired. Burnside, according to one historian, became a mere transmitter of McClellan's commands while Cox, because of Burnside's presence, probably felt his liberty to direct the *IX Corps* constrained. As a result, he proved reluctant to perform certain actions that he might have done otherwise such as personally inspecting the Antietam's fords for their suitability as crossing points.

This weakness in command was supplemented by another at the next echelon, the divisional level. The *IX Corps* had lost some key experienced and determined divisional commanders in the previous weeks, soldiers whose diligence, drive and inspiration would be sorely missed in the battle to come. Of Burnside's divisional commanders at Sharpsburg, all had obtained division command only weeks before the battle and two after long periods of inaction. Former brigade commander Orlando Willcox had taken over the *1st Division* after General Isaac Stevens's death. Willcox came to his position after a year in Confederate captivity. Isaac Rodman who was placed in charge of the *3rd Division* had been out of commission since spring, retiring from his post as a regimental commander due to illness. He took over the *3rd Division* from John Parke who in turn became Burnside's chief of staff. Brigadier General Samuel Sturgis, who moved into the vacancy in the *2nd Division* made by Jesse Reno's death, at least had been on active duty throughout the Union's dark days of August. The

General Samuel Sturgis led the Union *2nd Division*, *IX Corps*, which he only had recently taken over after Jesse Reno was killed at the battle of South Mountain.

Kanawha Division fell under the direction of a mere colonel, Eliakim Scammon. Overall, the assumption of divisional command by such novices on the eve of a great campaign could not have proved a boon to the *IX Corps'* fighting efficiency and its ability to meet the many tasks that lay ahead.

One of the most important of those tasks was also the most innocuous, finding a route across the Antietam's shallow waters. McClellan visited with Burnside on the night of the 16th to tell his subordinate of the *IX Corps'* role. The most obvious crossing point was the Lower Bridge, but the narrow span should have seemed more of an impediment than an attraction to the Federal advance. It was a potential bottleneck for a large assaulting column and the unfortunate soldiers ordered to cross it would be easy targets for Toombs's Georgians, well-protected in their entrenchments on the western bank's bluffs. Despite this obvious obstacle, Burnside did not labor to find an alternative. His command had been near the Lower Bridge since 15 September but little reconnaissance was conducted to find alternative routes. Captain James C. Duane gathered topographical information and forwarded this knowledge to commanders when they received their general orders. Only two fords were known before the attack, one to the north of the Lower Bridge, between it and the Middle Bridge, and another farther to the south of the Lower Bridge. Even after engineers found fording points two-thirds of a mile downstream, the primary focus of the Federal assault remained the bridge. General Cox insisted that this attention was only meant to pin down the forces that were in opposition there. The effort that was spent keeping the Georgians in place across the stream was considerable enough to belie that claim.

The *IX Corps'* lack of diligence in finding alternate fording points was a symptom of a greater sickness plaguing McClellan's entire army. As the events at Sharpsburg would show, spontaneity and vigor were qualities seriously lacking in the upper echelons of the *IX Corps*.

Burnside and Cox's divisions set up on the battle's eve

The narrowness of the Lower Bridge can be seen in this modern-day photo. McClellan and his officers ignored this obvious obstacle for a large assaulting force using the bridge to cross the river under enemy fire.

with Rodman's division on the far left on a country road leading toward the ford where it would cross the Antietam. Cox intended the march of this division to play a major role in unhinging the Confederate forces obstructing the bridge. Sturgis's division would advance against the bridge itself and was on both sides of the Lower Bridge Road with Willcox's division, the *IX Corps* reserve, behind it. The *Kanawha Division* had been split so that Scammon's brigades were paired with Rodman's, following them in support, and Crook was operating with Sturgis. Burnside took a hand in the day's offensive by directing Crook to lead the assault on the bridge the next day in honor of his command's good service at South Mountain. The *IX Corps* also had a formidable artillery force of several batteries on hand. Five of these were on the high ground slightly southeast of the bridge, arrayed with a wide range of pieces: Lieutenant

Samuel N. Benjamin's *2nd U.S. Artillery, Battery A* armed with 20-pound Parrot Rifles along with a section of Captain Seth J. Simmond's *Kentucky Light Artillery*; Lieutenant Charles P. Muhlenberg's *5th U.S. Artillery, Battery A* with its 12-pound Napoleons; Captain Jacob Roemer's *Battery L* of the *2nd New York Artillery* with its Ordnance Rifles; and Captain Asa Cook's *8th Battery* of the *Massachusetts Light Artillery* fighting with James Rifles and howitzers.

After 0700, an hour after the *I Corps* had launched the Federal assault, Cox received an order issued by McClellan through Burnside, the first of several commands from the *Army of the Potomac*'s commander to get the surly Burnside into action. In response to the command, the *IX Corps* took the high ground east of the Antietam valley, its troops being placed where they could find cover. Minute after minute ticked away as the *IX Corps* awaited further directives, its commanders watching the battle's course off to the north from Burnside's headquarters at the Henry Rohrbach farm, located on a high knoll a half mile from the creek. Cox remembered of those moments:

> From our position we looked, as it were, down between the opposing lines as if they had been the sides of a street, and as

General Ambrose Burnside led the Union forces that would assail the Lower Bridge though Jacob Cox was actually the general in command on the field.

General Jacob Cox was given command of the *IX Corps* by Burnside. This was a difficult post for Cox due to the awkwardness of the feud between Burnside and McClellan. Cox was the general to whom Burnside passed McClellan's orders to take the Lower Bridge.

the fire opened we saw wounded men carried to the rear and stragglers making off. Our lines halted, and we were tortured with anxiety as we speculated whether our men would charge or retreat. The enemy occupied lines and fences and stone-walls, and their batteries made gaps in the National ranks. Our long-range guns were immediately turned in that direction and we cheered every well-aimed shot. One of our shells blew up a caisson close to the Confederate line.

The *IX Corps* leadership would not remain mere observers for long. After 0910, around the time French's division was assaulting the Sunken Road, Colonel Delos P. Sackett rode up to the officers and handed Burnside the paper containing his orders. McClellan directed Burnside to carry the bridge and the heights on opposite bank of Antietam and then march on to Sharpsburg and the Confederate rear.

According to Cox, Burnside passed the information on to him immediately. Cox hurried from the Rohrbach farm to supervise his troops's bridge assault. The plan for the *IX Corps'* assault was to have the 440 men of the *11th Connecticut Regiment* under Colonel H. W. Kingsbury lead a bridge assault as skirmishers, followed by Colonel George Crook's *2nd Brigade* of the *Kanawha Division* supported by Sturgis's *2nd Division*. The original hope was to negate the Confederate advantages in terrain with supporting fire. Artillery was ready for that purpose and infantry was to be engaged in that task as well with Sturgis's division advancing to the plowed hill southeast of the bridge. From there they could fire on the enemy as the *11th Connecticut* and Crook's brigade made a rush from the high ground east of the bridge, crossed the bridge, fanned out to the north and south, and then moved forward to seize the heights beyond.

By now, nearly four hours after the *Army of the Potomac* had begun to lash out at Lee's force, the *IX Corps* had lost its opportunity to take a role in pinning down the Confederate forces that opposed it in the beginning of the day. Walker's division and Anderson's brigade were already playing their part in ravaging Sedgwick's *II Corps* division. With that chance lost, another had been gained. The general failure to make a breakthrough against the Confederate left increased incrementally McClellan's reliance on what the *IX Corps* could achieve, and it could achieve much. All the Federals had to do was get across the Antietam, a simple task on its face, but disturbingly difficult for the *IX Corps* leadership. For the next few hours, McClellan and the *IX Corps'* commanders focused their attention on the Lower Bridge.

CHAPTER 4

ATTACK OF THE 11TH CONNECTICUT AND CROOK'S MISSTEP

AS A NATIVE OF THE SHARPSBURG AREA and a staff officer under Stonewall Jackson during the battle of Antietam, Kyd Douglas had a keen perspective on the conflict that took place near his native soil. Douglas was of the firm belief that the bridge and the Antietam Creek were no mean obstacles. He later caustically chided Burnside and his Federals for the difficulties they experienced trying to get across the stream, "It was no pass of Thermopylae. Go and look at it and tell me if you don't think Burnside and his corps might have executed a hop, skip, and a jump and landed on the other side. One thing is for certain, they might have waded it that day without getting their waist belts wet in any place." Douglas's assessment of the *IX Corps'* predicament is, perhaps, somewhat harsh. The Antietam valley in the vicinity of the Lower Bridge may appear quite pleasant to the casual observer, but hardly a worse crossing point of the creek could have been found for thousands of troops and their accoutrements.

Perhaps the primary difficulty faced by the *IX Corps* was the bridge itself. The Lower Bridge was a triple-arched work of solid craftsmanship made of limestone, capped with a parapet that also flanked its approaches. Some 125-feet long and 12-feet wide, capable of fitting only a few men standing abreast at a time, it was quite a formidable obstacle to a force of thousands of men. Moreover, the ground near the bridge was ill-suited for the all-out assaults that Burnside's command intended to launch. The land on the eastern bank of the Antietam Creek did not lend itself well to the maneuvers required of Civil War-style ranks, especially those required to get across such a cramped span. The valley of the Antietam was very narrow, limiting the number of troops that could get engaged and make a rush for the bridge. Federal formations had only a 250-foot belt of flat land running in-between the creek's flowing waters and a chain of short plateaus with thin tree cover to the east on which to operate. More important, there would be little shelter from the enemy fire coming from the opposite bank. The ground here was, for the most part, open, being plowed or stubble fields north and east of the Lower Bridge Road, offering little protection from the enemy fire that would have to be endured during the rush for the bridge. Besides some tree cover on the hill immediately east of the span, the only cover to be had near the bridge was from two wooden fences, one bordering the Lower Bridge Road, extending south perpendicularly from the eastern entrance of the bridge and a stone wall extending north from the bridge's mouth. Farther south, in-between the lanes leading to the Henry Rohrbach farm and Porterstown, fronting the Lower Bridge Road on the hill southeast of the bridge, was a trapezoidal parcel of plowed ground. Below this and the Rohrbach Farm Lane and west of a bend in the Antietam's course, nearly 400 yards from the bridge, was some concealment offered by a large cornfield, sloping down a hillside toward the stream, extending south over a depression.

The open line of advance and the difficulty in maneuvering troops in this area, all before an entrenched enemy at close range, literally made it a "Valley of Death." Cox bitterly remarked after the war, "No point of attack on the whole field was unpromising as this."

Perhaps the best option for the *IX Corps* would have been to avoid a direct assault across the bridge, yet this course proved no easy remedy. The only way to avoid crossing at the bridge was to locate fordable points above and below it, and that task took a considerable amount of time during 17

September. Until those points could be found, hundreds of *IX Corps* troops sought to get across the Lower Bridge and many of them were killed or wounded in a series of desperate attempts—only a single regiment made the first try, Colonel Henry Kingsbury's *11th Connecticut*.

At or around 1000, the blue-clad ranks of the *11th Connecticut* stepped off on their charge for the Lower Bridge. These were not green troops though they had yet to endure as much combat as other units in the Union ranks. What they may have lacked in battlefield experience, the troops of the *11th Connecticut* made up in training.

Kingsbury and his *11th Connecticut* leapt out from their wooded cover into the open southeast of the bridge and headed obliquely northwest toward the bridge. Almost immediately Kingsbury's men came under an increasingly fierce and telling fire from the entrenched Georgians. For some reason the *IX Corps* planners initially did not seek to reduce the amount of time they would expose their troops to enemy fire and the troops from the Nutmeg State suffered for this absence of fortitude. The storm of bullets

The view across the Antietam that the Georgia troops had of the area approaching the Lower Bridge. Many Union soldiers lost their lives as the entrenched Georgians picked them off from their high position.

quickly whittled a number of men from the ranks as they continued to rush onward. Able to reach the bridge and the bank, the command spread out, seeking cover behind the wood fence along the Lower Bridge Road, south of the span, and the stone wall to the north of it. The survivors of the grueling dash began returning some shots to the opposite side of the stream against the enemy that had thus far punished them so harshly.

When Crook's supporting force failed to appear, it was cruelly apparent that the *11th Connecticut* could not carry the bridge on its own. Still, some of the unit's members struggled in vain to make an alternative path across the Antietam. One of those who made the attempt was a sensitive and refined officer with the regiment's *Company A*, Captain John D. Griswold, a Yale graduate from Lyme. Griswold audaciously undertook his own assault after the rest of the regiment had stalled, leading any of his troops that would follow over the eastern bank, seeking to wade to the other side of the Antietam. The young officer's ill-fated bravado might have been intended to inspire his comrades to continue forward, driven in part by romantic notions inspired by his classical education. Whatever the cause of his rashness, its result was inevitable. Griswold and the Connecticut soldiers that went with him were made even more vulnerable and inviting as targets as they negotiated through the stream's flowing waters than they had been on dry land. Several pitched into the Antietam wounded or dead. Confederate bullets hit Captain Griswold himself, injuring him severely, but he summoned up enough strength to make his way to the opposite bank. There he collapsed in his drenched uniform, bleeding, alone in-between the firing lines.

Those of the *11th Connecticut* who remained at the bridge may have had more protection behind the fences than Griswold had enjoyed crossing the creek, but they continued to suffer severely under the enemies' blazing fusillades. In just 15 minutes after beginning the engagement, the regiment lost 21 killed, 88 wounded, and 28 men as prisoners.

Among those who had fallen in the assault was the *11th Connecticut's* own commander himself, Colonel Kingsbury, hit four times while cheering on his men during their deadly work. His mortally wounded body was retrieved and carried back to the Rohrbach House. Among those who would mourn Colonel Kingsbury's passing was his brother-in-law, Brigadier General David R. Jones, the very commander of the troops that had cut him down.

The sacrifice of Kingsbury and the *11th Connecticut* proved in vain. The support for which they had provided skirmish fire never appeared on the field when and where they were needed. Only a fraction of Crook's brigade had arrived to fight alongside the them. Even before the *11th Connecticut* had gotten involved in the fight, Crook had dispatched two *11th Ohio* companies to the wooded hill overlooking the bridge. They settled down behind whatever cover they could find and engaged in a firefight with the entrenched enemy across the stream while the *11th Connecticut* made a charge to their left.

Crook's attack devolved into a fiasco shortly after he was ordered forward from his initial position northeast of the Rohrbach Farm, some time before the *11th Connecticut's* defeat. Somehow Crook had no knowledge that Burnside had conferred the honor of taking the bridge upon him and his troops. Whether the officer misunderstood his orders or they had been miscommunicated to him, the record is unclear. Instead, he was operating under a reversal of roles, believing his brigade would cross the span only after Sturgis's division had seized it. Crook must have been quite unsettled when he reached the Rohrbach Farm to find Sturgis and his men were nowhere in sight.

Faced with a muddled situation, Crook made a muddled response that ended up scattering his forces throughout the Rohrbach Farm. First he sent the *11th Ohio* companies forward to skirmish at the bridge. Next he left the *36th Ohio* in the orchard near the Rohrbach house as a reserve while he edged his forces around 250 yards east down the Rohrbach Farm Lane with the remainder of the brigade. At this point he dispatched four companies of the *28th Ohio* toward the bridge. These came under enemy's view when they advanced over the wooded hill and were subjected to fierce blasts of musketry that sent them retreating for the rest of the brigade. Crook then spun off part of his force by having five companies of the *28th Ohio* assail the crest of the wooded hill with Simmond's guns, presumably to provide a covering fire for his assaulting forces. These included the *28th*'s other five companies and the remainder of the *11th Ohio*. Finally, Crook's brigade was ready to make its attack across the Lower Bridge.

Inexplicably, Crook's force managed to fly apart in three different directions. Crook himself with the *28th*'s companies detailed to make the assault managed to get completely lost, missing the Lower Bridge entirely, and reaching the stream 350 yards north of his objective. There, his command tussled with an enemy force, perhaps members of the 20th Georgia, who had peppered the Ohioans with musketry. The Yankees sought cover to fire back, some behind one of the area's ubiquitous farm fences and a sandy ridge while the more fainthearted fled west for the relative safety of the Rohrbach Orchard. Though it is doubtful that the Confederate force was substantial, especially given the poverty of Jones's manpower, the fighting evidently became quite severe, or at least appeared so to Crook and his men who blasted away most of their ammunition. As Cox described the contest, "The engagement was one in which the Antietam prevented the combatants from coming to close quarters, but it was none the less vigorously continued with musketry fire." At any rate, the fusillades were enough to keep Crook's men from rejoining the contest for the bridge.

The *11th Ohio*, meanwhile, actually did manage to go where it was supposed to, but even its advance was tainted by the confusion inflicting Crook's command. Incredibly, the unit split in two shortly after it began to move forward. The right part headed toward the wooded hill where it joined the regiment's companies that had been sent there earlier in the day. The left, along with its commander Lieutenant Colonel Augustus Coleman, headed down the plowed hill into a ferocious enemy fire. Coleman initially accompanied his men incautiously riding a horse until advised to dismount lest he prove too attractive a target. The officer complied only to suffer a mortal wound. Regimental command devolved to Major Lyman Jackson who penned a report of Coleman's fatal injury and the *11th Ohio*'s involvement three days after the battle:

> We were ordered and led by Lieutenant-Colonel Coleman, then commanding the regiment, to move toward a bridge across the Antietam Creek then occupied by the enemy. I don't know the duty assigned, but two of our companies had been sent forward as skirmishers to the woods and hill-side on our side of the creek, I suppose it was to support them. Advancing in line across a plowed field and hill, the right and left divided, under conflicting orders, the right moving to our skirmishers forward on the right, the left moving to the base of hill by the creek. Lieutenant-Colonel Coleman, moving with the left under a severe fire was shot through the right arm by a sharpshooter, and died in about an hour after. I must say of him that no better, braver, truer officer ever served our country, and no regiment can feel a loss more sorely.

The enemy's fire proved too much to bear as Horton Teverbaugh, a first lieutenant in the *11th Ohio*'s *Company F* recalled, "Skirmishers were thrown out, and the column moved forward. Simmon[d]s' and McMullen's batteries were raining their deadly misses among the rebels' ranks, who in turn sent volley after volley from their muskets and artillery in the faces of our advancing troops. Bravely they struggled forward, but in vain. The steady stream of canister poured from the rebel cannon forced the line to waver, and finally to fall back." Major Jackson, realizing his current position was a futile one, ordered a retreat and headed to the wooded hill where his force rejoined the other companies of the regiment. These were re-formed and then turned against the enemy and they fired away there until their ammunition was exhausted. Meanwhile, Crook's unanticipated engagement was finally beginning to show some success.

Crook had finally found favorable conditions to push the *28th Ohio*'s companies with him across the Antietam. First, he was able to count on additional fire power from one of Simmond's guns lobbing double charges of canister at the enemy opposing him. Second, a suitable crossing for Crook's was located north of his current position. With this breakthrough, Crook now decided to concentrate that part of his brigade still east of the bridge for taking the Lower Bridge. Simmond's guns were pointed toward the bridge and the *36th Ohio* was called out of reserve to make the assault with the *11th Ohio*'s survivors.

These aggressive orders proved to be the disappointing denouement to Crook's involvement in the bridge attacks. By the time his troops were ready, the bridge had already been taken. Instead of playing a vital role in the span's seizure, Crook's *Kanawha* brigade had spent three hours wasting its ammunition in its disorganized movements and desultory fighting across the field. The honor of taking the bridge had gone to Sturgis's division, though not without a considerable cost in bloodshed.

CHAPTER 5

THE ATTACK OF NAGLE'S BRIGADE

THE *IX CORPS'* FIRST ATTACK AT SHARPSBURG had been a fiasco, costly not only in terms of the men engaged and lost, but in the additional troops required to be brought to bear against Toombs's and Benning's Georgians. With the mangling of the *11th Connecticut,* and part of Crooks's brigade involved in a fight of its own farther to the north, Burnside and Cox called upon another *IX Corps* force to take the bridge—the men of Sturgis's *2nd Division.*

The commission of this command was a fateful move. Burnside and Cox had originally intended that Sturgis's two brigades follow up any success obtained by Crook's Ohioans. To do this, these commands had moved up to the ground south of the bridge, took cover in the cornfield and behind the heights east of the bridge, where they could make quick use of the road in making for the other side. Now the *2nd Division*'s mission was to seize the Lower Bridge itself. The extent to which Sturgis's regiments exhausted their manpower and ammunition driving off the enemy on the opposite bank also weakened this large force's ability to participate in any offensive west of the Antietam.

Sturgis gave the necessary orders for the employment of Brigadier General James Nagle's *1st Brigade* with the command that its troops make their advance at the double-quick and with fixed bayonets. Nagle's brigade was a polyglot collection of regiments from various states: the *2nd Maryland, 6th* and *9th New Hampshire,* and *48th Pennsylvania.* The situation Nagle found before the Lower Bridge was not ideal, especially since his ability to organize his regiments for assault was cramped by the Antietam Creek's narrow valley. Negating this disadvantage required a more novel approach than had been previously employed. Rather than take the course the *11th Connecticut* had used in their assault, Nagle chose to have his troops advance on the bridge by charging north up the Lower Bridge Road along the Antietam, a course hundreds of yards in length that would expose his troops to flanking fire from the Georgians on the bluffs opposite. Union troops stationed along the stream and the heights to the east would blast away at the entrenched enemy, attempting to suppress the Confederates from shooting apart the charge as it progressed northward up the Lower Bridge Road.

The *2nd Maryland* and *6th New Hampshire* were charged with the assault component of Nagle's plan while the *48th Pennsylvania* and *9th New Hampshire* were to offer the suppressing fire to protect their comrades' advance. As the troops organized for their duty, there is evidence Nagle may not have been up on the front lines to accompany them. There was not a high opinion of the commander among some New Hampshiremen. When a staff officer rode up to the ranks of the *6th New Hampshire* asking for the brigade commander, a soldier stiffly replied, "He's back there quiled up under a stune."

The staging ground for the attack was made in and near the cornfield south of the bridge where the troops put aside the burden of their backpacks to make ready for the charge. Colonel Jacob Eugene Duryee finished a conference with Sturgis and Nagle and approached his men in a gulch east of the cornfield, buttoning his blouse as he came, a sign that portended his regiment would soon be going into action. Sturgis had offered the officer a general's star if his Marylanders could take the bridge. The ambitious Duryee, eager to win the prize, rejoined his men and led them down the gulch toward the creek. During these moments of preparation, the *9th New Hampshire* suffered one of its first casualties when Private E. M. Messenger suffered a grievous but not mortal wound. Messenger would prove one of the luckier members of the regiment and brigade that day. Many others would not survive the coming charge.

While Nagle's *1st Brigade* prepared, all the Union artillery batteries east of the stream were belching forth their deadly missives, pounding the entrenched enemy positions. The *48th Pennsylvania* was the first to go into motion. Its path first went over the plowed hill and then over to the wooded hill where it took the place of the *11th Ohio* which was rendezvousing with the *36th Ohio* in the Rohrbach orchard. From these heights it added its own fire to that of the artillery's. The *2nd Maryland* and *6th New Hampshire* meanwhile had their stepping off point fixed behind the plowed hill.

At about 1130, Nagle's men, with bayonets fixed as ordered, marched off on their own assault against the bridge, almost an hour and half after the *11th Connecticut*'s assault. The *2nd Maryland* and *6th New Hampshire* made their way over the plowed ground north of the cornfield to master the first obstacle in their march, the wooden fence bordering the field and the Lower Bridge Road. Officers ran ahead to take down some of the fence planks and make an opening for the attacking troops. At first the Rebel positions were ominously silent when the Federal ranks came into view, as if waiting to spring a trap on an unwary quarry. The quiet did not last long. With the suddenness of a thunderclap, the Georgians' muskets exploded in a volley of musketry as Nagle's men began to tear at the fence rails to clear their way. The dead and wounded quickly began to fall into the earthen furrows as their comrades pushed against the stubborn fence. Officers, seeing their beleaguered commands in danger of collapsing, vociferously sought to keep the troops pressing onward. Duryee himself urged his men on, his voice cutting above the combat's din, "What the hell you doing there? Straighten that line there forward." At his command, the regiment indeed filed into order and pressed on into the road heading toward the

A modern photo of the route Nagle's troops took as they approached the Lower Bridge. The fence was the first obstacle they encountered and it slowed their advance until they could get over or through it while under enemy fire.

bridge. Confederate artillery had opened on the Marylanders by this time, one shot killing a captain by shaving off the top of his head. The Rebel infantry located on the bluffs above their quarry were almost invited to deliver a destructive flanking fire, their targets moving below their position and parallel to it only 100 yards distant. The *6th New Hampshire* was the next of Nagle's regiments to take up the charge, its ranks too suffering heavy casualties.

Once again a Federal attack against the Lower Bridge was stalling under the galling Georgian fire and collapsing into a miserable bloody failure. About one-third of the Marylanders had fallen, but they still pressed forward to within 250 feet of the bridge before they began to fall apart completely. Unable to continue, the *2nd Maryland* and *6th New Hampshire* at first halted to shoot back at the enemy, a vain act of defiance given their exposed position. Seeking better cover the regiments retreated for the hills east of the bridge. Behind them lay scores of dead and wounded. The *2nd Maryland* lost 67 men during the day, the highest loss in Nagle's brigade. Sixty fell out of the *6th New Hampshire*'s ranks.

The *9th New Hampshire* remained in action below the bridge, firing away, taking position behind the wooden fence bordering the road. Despite the smaller numbers of the enemy facing them, the Yankees vividly recounted that they endured a near torrential fire before and during their engagement on the Lower Bridge Road. According to the *9th New Hampshire*'s historian, the Confederate fusillades completely terrified one comrade so much that he was simply paralyzed: "Just as the regiment was getting into position at the rail fence, the man fell flat on the ground. 'Get up!' shouted the captain. 'I can't' said the man; and the captain finally ordered some of the men to lay him under the bank, where he wouldn't get hit. The next day the man reported for duty. He had been completely prostrated by nervous excitement." A member of the *9th New Hampshire*'s *Company F* told that he and his comrades found that Rebel musketry was not the only deadly missives causing concern, they also suffered a rain of railroad iron fired from enemy cannon. A large piece, almost 15 inches long, had whizzed close by this soldier's head and tumbled over the ground nearby. In the midst of the fray, one of the *9th New Hampshire*'s officer's took up a rifle, according to a regimental letter to the Lebanon, New Hampshire's *Free Press*, only to suffer unfortunate consequences: "Lieutenant Colonel [H. B.] Titus seized the gun of a man who fell by his side, and used it through most of the fight, until a Minie ball from a rebel sharpshooter struck him in the side and entered his shoulder producing a severe wound, and he was taken from the field."

The *9th* evidently made a grand display during their involvement in this phase of the battle. Brigade commander Nagle specifically commended the New Hampshiremen in his report: "The Ninth New Hampshire Volunteers, Col.

E. Q. Fellows, was placed near the bridge and opened a destructive fire directly upon the enemy and expended nearly all their ammunition during a gallant resistance of an hour, in which they were between the fires of two regiments of the enemy, and sustained themselves nobly." Despite their gallantry, the enemy fire proved too tough for the New Hampshiremen, who running low on ammunition were also forced to seek cover behind the hill east of the bridge.

But the men of the *9th New Hampshire* and their fellows did not find they were completely safe on and behind the ridge. Enemy artillery were still in the business of hurling death in their direction and soldiers could easily fall victim to it if they were not careful.

Some troops traded shots with enemy troops on the opposite side of the bank. A Sergeant Rand of the *6th New Hampshire's Company K* wanted to get into the act when he spotted W. W. French hurriedly loading and firing his musket at targets across the stream. Rand told French he was a "good shot" and requested the soldier load rifles while he took a turn at firing them. The bargain struck, Rand took a spot behind a tree, picked an inviting subject and leaned out a bit beyond his cover to get a better view. This lack of caution proved the end of the sergeant. A quicker Confederate sharpshooter put a bullet through Rand's forehead, his lifeless body collapsing on French and both men rolling a short distance down the hill. Unphased, French picked himself up and made for cover where he returned to the business of firing on the enemy.

By the time the assault of Nagle's brigade had folded, it was noon on the battlefield and both sides blasted away at each other from their positions along the creek. The musketry was nearly continuous according to one of the *9th New Hampshire's* veterans, " . . . for more than two hours one continued roll of musketry was kept up along the lines, the rebels having the advantage of high ground and a narrow piece of heavy woodland as a breastwork. The contest was desperate."

CHAPTER 6

ATTACK OF FERRERO'S BRIGADE

THE IX CORPS' CONTINUED FAILURE to take the bridge was proving increasingly disconcerting to Major General McClellan. Word had come to his headquarters that the bridge was still in enemy hands despite his urgent command that it be carried at all hazards. Since dispatches alone had failed to encourage Burnside's prompt seizure of the bridge across the Antietam, the senior general sent Colonel Sackett back to Burnside's headquarters. This time Sackett would remain with Burnside as insurance that the taking of the bridge would finally be achieved. Sackett carried another urgent message from McClellan ordering Burnside to seize the bridge speedily, with the bayonet if necessary. Sackett's arrival only augmented Burnside's ire against his commanding officer. Still, he forwarded McClellan's messages on to Cox and even took a more direct role in the battle by communicating with division commander Sturgis. Both Cox and Burnside were eagerly awaiting some word from Rodman on his quest to ford the Antietam, hopeful that his efforts might prevent the need for another direct assault against the enemy's strong position, or at least alleviate the pressure faced. Such news was not forthcoming. Once again, another force would have to be hurled toward the Lower Bridge to drive across it and seize the ground beyond.

The next IX Corps brigade summoned to break the deadlock at the bridge was Sturgis's 2nd Brigade under Brigadier General Edward Ferrero. Ferraro's command boasted the 21st and 35th Massachusetts, the 51st New York, and the 51st

Pennsylvania. While Ferrero's brigade was in motion toward the field, the men could hear the distant din of Nagle's brigade's desperate attempt to gain the bridge. The history of the *35th Massachusetts* includes this reminiscence, "It was near eleven o'clock, and a brisk contest had been going on for some time upon the creek below us, but the trees and smoke concealed all from view. We could hear our men shouting, and their foes yelling, amid the rattle of small arms; it seemed hot work down there." The brigade had been stationed in the cornfield southeast of the bridge before they took their part in the assaults against the bridge. There the troops had encountered the human cost of the failed attempts that had gone before them—the broken bodies of wounded soldiers tending to their injuries. The history of the *35th* recalled, "At length the order came for us to move forward. We descended the hill by the left flank, and passed between the stalks of tall corn on the level, meeting several men holding an arm or some other member from which red blood was dripping. The air was close and stifling."

The sound of desperate fighting and the sight of its aftermath probably caused some anxiety among the green troops of the *35th Massachusetts* when they learned that they were to be put in the thick of the fighting. On the march, the men of the *35th* overheard the task in store for them when an aide approached General Sturgis to make an inquiry for Ferrero: "Colonel Ferrero wishes to know what to do with the regiments," he said. Sturgis replied, "Have him move the regiments (the three older ones) down the stream immediately and take the bridge!" When asked what was to be done with the *35th*, the aide was told, "Tell him to move it across the bridge and up the hill in line of battle. There must be no delay; General Burnside is waiting for this to be done now!" The aide pointed out that the *35th*'s objective would be a dangerous one. "Is artillery aimed at that position?" he inquired. "Yes," Sturgis responded, "but that shall be stopped." The rookie *35th Massachusetts* prepared for the daunting task ahead by shedding their packs and stacking them on the ground. A sentry was detailed to guard over the pile, proof that the Massachusetts men had learned a lesson on life in the *Army of the Potomac* the hard way. When they had gone into battle at South Mountain, soldiers had left behind their packs unattended, returning later to find some dishonorable thieves had made off with them.

As Ferrero's brigade awaited orders, a member of the *51st Pennsylvania* earned a painful distinction while conducting a personal reconnaissance of the enemy position. Captain Parker wrote, "Lieut. John J. Freedley, R.Q.M., ventured to the top of a hill that overlooked the rebel batteries, to gratify his curiosity in knowing the rebels' position. He, however, was satisfied, for he only had been there a moment when a shell from a rebel gun exploded a little above him, a piece of which struck him in the shoulder, inflicting a painful wound. He was taken to the rear and his wound attended to." The rest of the regiment prepared themselves for the task at hand.

Colonel Ferrero, himself, rode forward to the soldiers of the *51st Pennsylvania* and the *51st New York* to rouse their spirits for the difficult task they had been charged to undertake. The memorable exchange between the brigade commander and the Pennsylvanian troops has gone down in Civil War lore as the famous "whiskey" episode. The incident was recounted by Captain Parker:

> "Attention, second brigade!" Quick as a flash the brigade was "in line." He then rode up in front of the colors of the 51st P.V., and spoke to the men as follows: "It is General Burnside's special request that the two 51sts take that bridge. Will you do it?" The request was unlooked for and the men had not time to think of it, when Corporal Lewis Patterson, of Co. I, although a temperate man, exclaimed, "Will you give us our whiskey, Colonel, if we take it?" Col. Ferrero turned suddenly around to the corporal and replied, Yes, by G–, you shall have as much as you want, if you take the bridge. I don't mean the whole brigade, but you two regiments shall have just as much as you want, if

it is in the commissary or I have to send to New York to get it, and pay for it out of my own private purse; that is, if I live to see you through it. Will you take it? A unanimous "Yes," went up that told of the determination of the men to take the bridge . . .

Evidently some members of the *51st Pennsylvania* had become quite notorious for their ability to locate and quaff the intoxicating beverage. Whiskey was quite an incentive, but Captain Parker optimistically, if not credulously, contended that Ferrero's promise was not the prime consideration of the troops when making the charge. Instead, he argued that a desire to prove worthy of General Burnside's confidence primarily fueled the determination of the *51st Pennsylvania* and the *51st New York* regiments. In preparation for their part, the men laid aside their packs in the cornfield and filled their canteens at a nearby spring.

The assault by the twin *51sts* would take a different tack than that employed by its unfortunate predecessors. Evidently the high cost of the day's failures had made some impression on the *IX Corps* leadership. Rather than approach the bridge from the south as Nagle's brigade had done or from the southeast along a path similar to that the *11th Connecticut* had taken, the *2nd Brigade's* regiments would move off from that part of the hill directly across from the bridge, reducing the flanking fire the enemy could throw against them. The Pennsylvanians would be on the right and the New Yorkers on the left of the attacking formation, overall some 770 men. In preparation for their charge, Ferrero's brigade moved through the cornfield on the Lower Bridge Road and then, all the time being pelted by musketry, grapeshot, and canister, marched north getting behind Nagle's troops on the hills east of the bridge. The 150-man strong *21st Massachusetts* was detached to the western front of the valley's plowed field. From this position they could better provide covering fire against the enemy at close range while behind the protection of the wood fence found there. The green troops of the *35th Massachusetts* followed the *51sts* to the top of

the hills east of the bridge. Nagle's infantry would participate as well by offering a supporting fire from their positions on the eastern bank. Simmond's guns were now
trained on the Georgians and other batteries had been
brought closer to the Antietam's bank to fire canister and
shell at close range.

At 1230, the Pennsylvanians and New Yorkers took their
turn at braving the ferocity of the Confederate fire as they
made a 300-yard dash for the Lower Bridge. The enemy's
continued barrage of cannon and musketry again proved
too powerful for the attacking forces, splintering the
oncoming formations, negotiating over the bodies of their
predecessors, forcing their numbers to initially seek shelter
rather than continue their charge headlong over the bridge.
The *51st New York* took a detour south of the bridge to seek
cover behind the wooden fence there, bordering the eastern
side of the Lower Bridge Road, while the Pennsylvanians
took shelter behind the stone wall to the north. As Captain
Parker tells it, the regiments turned to blasting away at the
entrenched enemy beyond the stream, ". . . they laid under
cover of the wall and opened a terrific fire of musketry on
the enemy, who were snugly ensconced in their rude but
substantial breastworks, in quarry holes, behind high ranks
of cord-wood, logs, stone popels, &c., making it too hot a
place for the enemy to be in, and too close for further resistance. They began to withdraw from their position by twos
and threes, singly, and in whatever way they could with
the most safety to themselves." Indeed, the Georgians were
finally pulling out, though the reasons were a mite more
complex than the fusillades from the *51sts*.

In fact, the *51sts* were operating under an advantage that
their comrades in the *11th Connecticut* and Nagle's brigade
had lacked; Toombs's and Benning's Georgian troops had
been slowly worn down by attrition. Despite their ability to
fend off direct attacks, they had now been engaged for
nearly three hours during which their already slim numbers had taken many casualties from the near continual
Federal infantry fire and artillery shelling. Ammunition

The *51st New York* and *51st Pennsylvania* charge over the Lower Bridge as the Union finally broke the Confederate hold. (*Harper's Weekly*)

was also running low and efforts to get more had proven perilous.

More importantly, according to the Confederate officers who claimed they could have held the bridge otherwise, Federal efforts to cross the Antietam elsewhere had finally come to fruition. To the north Crook's troops of the *28th Ohio* had pressed across the stream scattering the enemy that had harassed them for so long. To the south, Rodman had managed to find a ford that would enable his men to get across the Antietam and was pressing northward toward the rear of the Confederates defending the bridge. Under pressure from nearly all sides, Toombs wisely decided to retreat for the main Confederate line to the west.

With the Georgians beginning to retreat for the rear, the Federals in the *51st New York* and *51st Pennsylvania* saw the chance to accomplish the mission so many men had given their lives and blood to achieve. One of the first to realize the opportunity was the *51st New York's* commander, Colonel Potter. As the Confederate fire began to slacken, the officer spotted Confederates falling back and soon afterward, he ordered his men to get across the bridge, waving them on with his sword. The Pennsylvanians also realized the time had come to seize the span and poured across as well. As Captain Parker told the story, the soldiers of the *51st Pennsylvania* were forced to go through some difficult maneuvering to get over the span.

Captain Allebaugh, who commanded Co. C, (the color company,) now resolved that the time had come to take the bridge, and the regiment prepared for the final struggle that was either to make them the victors or the vanquished. Colonel Hartranft gave the final orders for the successful accomplishment of the desperate task which now lay before it. As the regiment made the charge, Captain Allebaugh led his company at double-quick towards a gateway leading out of the field into the road that crossed the bridge, but on nearing the gate his company became the target of the concentrated fire of the enemy on the opposite side of the stream. Here his first lieutenant was struck down and his men were

John Hartranft and his *51st Pennsylvanians* were some of the first Union troops to charge across the Lower Bridge.

falling at every step. He soon perceived his perilous situation and flew off at a tangent by "right oblique," and made a short detour from the gate to the abutment of the bridge, and rushed across the bridge . . .

With both the New Yorkers and the Pennsylvanians charging over the bridge, their flags nearly side by side, the cheering regiments became a tangled mass of men jammed on the narrow passage so that a halt had to be called to sort out their ranks. A frustrated Colonel Potter jumped up on the bridge's parapet cursing the situation. Potter's comrade, Colonel Hartranft of the *51st Pennsylvania*, also took a role urging on his men. According to Captain Parker, "Colonel Hartranft cheered on his men in the assault until he became so exhausted that he could not make himself heard, and as he reached the bridge he said, 'Come on, boys, for I can't halloo any more,' but kept waving his hat in the air as encouragement to keep on across." The crowd eventually continued past the western mouth of the bridge and up onto the bluffs beyond. Some New Yorkers tried the alternative method of fording the stream itself, now a considerably safer enterprise than when Captain Griswold had attempted it. Finally, Federal troops had managed to secure a foothold on the western mouth of the bridge. Ecstatic elation and relief swept through the ranks at the news.

Soon other *IX Corps* regiments were running pell-mell for the western side of the Antietam. The *35th Massachusetts* received its command directly from Colonel Fererro, who told aide Lieutenant John Hudson, "Hudson, tell your colonel to cross the bridge immediately, move along the road to the right, form in line and advance up the hill." The lieutenant met his charge and with the commands "Forward" and "Double quick!" the regiment was on its way toward the bridge. The history of the regiment tells what happened next when they reached open ground:

Here was a startling scene of battle; clouds of smoke overhung; along the creek below the bridge. The Twenty First Massachusetts and our Company A were actively engaged with the enemy posted behind the trees, rails and stones upon the rocky acclivity across the stream; dead and wounded men in blue lay about, some still tossing and writhing in their agony; the bridge was filled with men of the Fifty-First Pennsylvania and Fifty-First New York, who had preceded us, some kneeling behind the parapets of the bridge and firing up at the gray coats, others crowding forward up to the farther end of the bridge and also firing upward.

Our regiment came partly into line, as if to open fire along the back of the bridge; then by the column's commands, swung by the right again and joined the throng, hurrying on to the further bank, the third regiment to cross. Confederate sharpshooter dropped or slid from overhanging trees in which they had been hidden—one clinging to a branch the moment he fell. It is said that Colonel Ferraro seized a musket and fired among them. In a shorter time than it takes to tell it we had crowded across the bridge and filed into the road to the right, where the two regiments that had preceded us were halted. The line of the regiment was formed quickly and steadily, facing up the hill, which here rose more gently than below the bridge.

Oliver Bosbyshell, historian of the *48th Pennsylvania*, told of his unit's rush over the bridge with the rest of Nagle's brigade following soon afterwards. Unlike Ferrero's brigade, the *48th* headed to the left on the western bank and filed up a narrow lane up onto the bluffs. According to Bosbyshell, ". . . the bridge was wrested from the enemy and almost immediately came the command, 'Forward,' and the Forty-eighth rushed down the hillside, over the bridge, up the steep declivity to the top of the bluffs, from which the enemy were fleeing at a rapid rate. Going up the steep road, the body of a rebel officer was seen propped up against a tree. 'Captain,' said Private Clem Evans, 'may I get that officer's sword?' The desired permission was given. He returned to the ranks with the trophy in a few moments, saying that he did not secure the belt because the man was not quite dead!"

The historian of the *9th New Hampshire* also gave an account of his unit's crossing: "Colonel Fellows, of the

Ninth, protected from the rays of the Maryland sun by an old-fashioned palm-leaf hat, was near the top of the ridge behind which his regiment lay, earnestly watching every maneuver. As the New York and Pennsylvania regiments drew upon themselves the terrible shower of Confederate Minnie balls, shells, cannon-balls, and railroad iron, Colonel Fellows saw his opportunity, and waving his hat as he shouted the order, 'Forward, Ninth New Hampshire! Follow the old palm-leaf!' he rushed into the fray and the Ninth New Hampshire was across the bridge before the enemy could again concentrate their fire!"

Together Nagle's regiments, the *48th Pennsylvania* and the *9th New Hampshire*, joined by the *6th Hampshire*, pushed forward west to a ridge overlooking the rolling ground south and east of Sharpsburg. There they came under the fire of Confederate troops that had remained behind to skirmish and distant batteries throwing forth barrages of shot and shell.

Expanding their bridgehead, the triumphant *IX Corps* Federals managed to sweep up some tardy Confederates in the process as prisoners. Some Confederates who had been trapped in their positions on the bluffs made makeshift flags of surrender by sticking newspaper shreds onto ramrods. Company D of the 2nd Georgia had not even heard orders to retreat over the deafening roar of artillery and musketry and many of their ranks were taken as a result. The men of the *35th Massachusetts* also came on some Confederates wishing to surrender, "Men in gray came down the hill, holding up both hands, or waving dirty white rags and were sent to the rear as prisoners."

One Confederate was reluctant to give up the struggle for the bridge. Lieutenant Colonel W. R. Holmes, the commander of the 2nd Georgia, called upon his men to follow him as he boldly rushed up to the Union ranks, waving his sword defiantly at the enemy. The gesture was reminiscent of Griswold's bravado earlier in the day and proved just as fatal. The Yankees leveled blasts of musketry in his direction and the Confederate colonel's lifeless body hit the ground riddled with bullets. Holmes's officers tried to recover the body only to have two fall wounded themselves and the rest gave up the attempt rather than become casualties as well. By this time Major Skidmore Harris, according to Toombs, was "the last remaining field officer" in this sector and half the 2nd Georgia were also casualties.

By 1300, the bridge was solidly in Federal hands and a foothold was held on the western bank of the Antietam. The fight for the bridge had cost 550 Federal soldiers while Toombs's Georgians had suffered 120 lost defending it. Cox gave this assessment of his casualty figure, "The proportion of casualties to the number engaged was much greater than common, for the nature of the task required that comparatively few troops should be exposed at once, the others remaining under cover." Another casualty was the loss in time. Three whole hours had passed trying to sweep aside the comparatively tiny command that opposed the Federal force. That a small number of Confederates had held up so many thousands of Burnside's force for so long was a credit to Toombs and Benning and their men, and a demerit staining the leadership of the *IX Corps*.

After crossing the bridge, more precious hours would again be spent preparing for the onslaught against Jones's main line yet to come. The *IX Corps'* final advance had assumed paramount importance since much of the other offensives of the *Army of the Potomac's* engagement against Lee's army to the north had run out of steam. Instead of coordinating the *IX Corps'* continued offensive with other Federal attacks elsewhere, it would continue on its own and would be the last, best chance to defeat the Confederates at Sharpsburg.

CHAPTER 7

RODMAN'S CROSSING AT SNAVELY'S FORD

WHILE THE STRUGGLE FOR THE LOWER BRIDGE raged on for hours, not far off to the south was the *IX Corps' 3rd Division,* formed of Colonel Harrison Fairchild's *1st Brigade,* Colonel Edward Harland's *2nd Brigade,* and Colonel Hugh Ewing's *1st Brigade* of the *Kanawha Division,* all searching for a fording point of the Antietam. It was a simple mission that the corps' leadership evidently had put much stock in. As Cox himself later wrote, "Burnside's view of the matter was that the frontal attack at the bridge was so difficult that the passage by the ford below must be an important factor in the task; for if Rodman's division should succeed in getting across there, at the bend of the Antietam, he would come up in the rear of Toombs, and wither the whole of D. R. Jones's division would have to advance to meet Rodman, or Toombs must abandon the bridge." Nevertheless, instead of playing a major role in the fighting as Burnside and Cox had envisioned, Rodman's command disappeared from the action only to reemerge during the final Federal assault on the lower bridge. The most formidable enemy obstructing the *3rd Division*'s trek was not Confederate opposition, but the difficult terrain south of the Lower Bridge, turning what was supposed to be a quick and easy march into a journey of several hours.

The commander charged with finding the lower ford, Brigadier General Isaac Rodman, met continuing frustration and several dispiriting mischances in his role at Sharpsburg. The search for the ford was merely the first of such depressing events. Supposedly, his *3rd Division*'s

General Isaac Rodman led the Union troops searching for a lower ford across Antietam Creek.

appointed crossing point had been determined a day before the battle by engineers with the *Army of the Potomac*. After Rodman's troops were ordered to advance around 1000 they made their way to the named fording point only to find to their frustration the point proved unsuitable to the division's needs. The banks there were much too steep to effect a crossing easily, a problem compounded by the presence of bluffs on the stream's eastern side. The realization that this ford would be impracticable came rather late in the day given a brigade from the division was supposed to be in position opposite the ford that morning. Another crossing needed to be found, a task that would delay Rodman's division's appearance on the field until shortly after noon, necessitating the several assaults on the Lower Bridge

Fortunately, Rodman learned from helpful local civilians that there was another crossing even farther downstream and decided to make an effort to locate the new point and cross there. Two companies of the *8th Connecticut*, entrusted with the mission of finding the ford, led the way. These troops made a difficult trek along the Antietam's course, fighting their way through trees and underbrush in the process while under a sniping fire from members of the

50th Georgia tracing their progress on the opposite bank of the Antietam.

The operation proved time consuming. The division had to make its way around the bend in the Antietam where the stream, after heading in a subtle southeastern path, veered sharply to the southwest, and then navigate the steep descents into the narrow valley. After a few hours of searching, the crossing point, called Snavely's Ford, was finally found. Though less than a mile directly southeast from the bridge, Rodman's division had to march two miles to get there. Only a handful of Confederate troops were on hand to contest the advance and these were easily sent scurrying away for safety. Even more time was lost as Rodman's division began to negotiate its crossing of the Antietam while under cover of Captain James R. Whiting's battery of five 12-pound Navy howitzers supported by the remainder of the *8th Connecticut's* infantry. By the time a column was marching down a winding path toward the stream, the *51st Pennsylvania* and *51st New York* were beginning their contest for the Lower Bridge.

The prospect of crossing at Snavely's must have been foreboding. Not only was water fairly deep and the current brisk at the crossing, but Confederate skirmishers were stationed not far away behind a stone wall, ready to snipe away at anyone making their way through the Antietam. The Yankees waded into the stream despite the dangers, Fairchild's brigade going first to be followed by Harland's, slowly crossing the stream for the opposite bank as bullets whizzed through the air and plopped into the water around them. Rodman's troops focused on getting across and refused to raise a rifle in reply. Once across, Fairchild's brigade headed up a northward bearing path along a steep bluff. They finally linked up with their *IX Corps* comrades by taking position on the left of Sturgis's men who had crossed the stream by the more direct route of the Lower Bridge.

At the head of Rodman's division during the crossing was the *9th New York*, notable by their very appearance as

A modern-day photo of the area around Snavely's Ford where some of the Union troops forded the Antietam.

a Zouave regiment, their uniforms deep blue in color with a scarlet sash, a fez and trimmings. Charles F. Johnson, one of the *9th Zouaves*, remembered the division's circuitous route to across the Antietam:

> An Aid came to General Rodman, and immediately after we ordered to "Attention" and sent down the fields toward the creek. The General procured a guide to show him the ford, and after many dubious windings and turning into woods, we came to what appeared to be rapids, and into this we plunged. Some Rebel sharpshooters discovered us and did not fail to scatter a few of their bullets from long range, but what damage was done was mostly from the bubbling waters. Out of the creek, we found the steep cliff before us, and with considerable difficulty, scrambled up here, and here we are. God only knows where we will be before the sun goes down.

The troops of the *9th New York* now awaited, many with fearful anticipation, their next part to play in the grand battle. Most had realized that the limited engagement at the ford was merely a prelude to an even greater confrontation in the future. It would be some time before their concerns were finally realized.

When Harland's brigade got onto the opposite side of the Antietam, it tended to the skirmishers that had been annoying the crossing. The Federals swept away the Confederates, with some assistance from Whiting's guns, and advanced to the west where some Confederate cavalry made their presence known. Their musketry, combined with Eshleman's Confederate battery hundreds of yards to the northwest, took some casualties from Harland's ranks, forcing the brigade to fall back and follow the path of Fairchild's men.

Ewing's men were next, crossing while being pelted with shrapnel fire from Eshleman's battery. These troops finally reached the Federal line west of the bridge around 1400. Whiting's artillery was last to cross only to find their cannon could not easily be transported over the difficult terrain nor could the battery's ammunition be brought across. Whiting's men found they had to recross the Antietam and backtrack all the way to the bridge to get on the western bank. Even after covering the distance to the bridge, they were not allowed to get their guns into action. Whiting's men kept rifles on hand since they were also used as infantry and it was for this purpose that Burnside himself decided to employ them when they met the general near the Lower Bridge. Whiting's guns were left behind under guard while his cannoneers were sent to Cox with their small arms and served as skirmishers throughout the rest of the day.

The majority of the *IX Corps* was now west of the Antietam, but everyone from Burnside and Cox to the rank and file would soon find that the many calamities enfeebling their ability to achieve victory were not all behind them.

CHAPTER 8

PREPARING FOR THE NEXT STAGE

FINALLY ACROSS THE LOWER BRIDGE, the *IX Corps'* advance stopped on the high ground just west of the span. The combined efforts made by Burnside's divisions in crossing the Antietam temporarily spent the force's ability to make a continued offensive. In particular, the units involved in the bridge's seizure, especially Sturgis's division, were exhausted from their labors and low on ammunition. The *51st Pennsylvania* on average could only count six cartridges to a man after the bridge action and many other units were not much better off. The situation was such that Brigadier General Cox later said it would have been "folly" to have pressed on, especially before reinforcements could arrive. While the wait to rest, reorganize, and receive supplies may have been wise, it took a considerable amount of time and again delayed the *IX Corps'* final move against the main Confederate position outside Sharpsburg until midafternoon.

Some units wanted to press on. The enthusiastic *35th Massachusetts* pressed ahead of the main body after crossing the bridge, coming under a particularly destructive bombardment from Confederate artillery. According to the *35th*'s history, "The regiment reached the bare brow of a hill west of the bridge—the first to appear there—and moved some distance by the right flank to the higher part of the rise. Before us, towards Sharpsburg, the enemy were scattering back to their artillery upon the hills on the hither side of the town. The hostile battery, which we had been watching an hour before, now, close at hand, opened on us at once, and sent the iron whizzing around us, shells taking effect in Companies D and H, cutting Luther F. Read in two, killing David W. Cushing and severely wounding Lieutenant Baldwin." When the regiment learned that Sturgis's division had halted due to lack of ammunition, the Massachusetts men made a reluctant retreat, passing over a farm fence, a move that caused concern among some who feared getting injured by their own comrades in the withdrawal: "Accordingly, our colonel, seeing no supports behind him, ordered the regiment to retire under the brow of the hill and lie down. The shells hurtled around us as we climbed the fence in retreat; yet many, indignant at the notion of falling back, and fearing more the bayonets of their compatriots while getting over the fence more than missiles of the enemy, waited a bit, until the line had crossed, before following." A friendly threat materialized from Union gunners who mistook the regiment as the enemy and began throwing some shells in its direction. Colonel Carruth waved his hat at the artillery in an attempt to stop the fire. When that did not work he ordered the color-bearers to wave their banners. The artillerists took notice and the *35th* returned to the main *IX Corps* line.

The *IX Corps* line that had formed on the western side of the Antietam had Sturgis's division forming the right with its right resting near the creek 300 yards north of the bridge. Crook's brigade was that division's support, the *28th Ohio*'s companies were reunited with the rest of the brigade that crossed the Antietam at the bridge. Rodman's division, supported by Ewing's brigade, formed the left flank extending south of the bridge. These Union ranks were strengthened by artillery when Durrell's *Pennsylvania Light, Battery D* and Clark's *4th United States, Battery E* came across the stream. These both set up on the left of the line northeast of the large 40-acre cornfield in-between the Antietam valley and the high ground along the Harper's Ferry Road.

Cox requested Burnside's remaining division—Willcox's—still three-quarters of a mile to the rear, to move forward and join the rest of the corps. This force would replace Sturgis's exhausted command and allow his troops to take their place as the *IX Corps'* reserve. Burnside immediately responded to Cox's request and Willcox had his troops on the move promptly to meet the order. Still, these new troops had a long way to go before their arrival and many obstacles in their path, not the least of which was the Lower Bridge. As early afternoon waned, the bridge that had helped impede the *IX Corps'* advance began to stagger Federal ranks once again. Crowds of troops vied to cross the narrow span with supply wagons, artillery pieces and caissons moving in the same direction. The *35th Massachusetts*, positioned near the Lower Bridge, witnessed Willcox's crossing there, "It was slow work passing Willcox's division . . . through the narrow defile of the stone bridge, only twelve feet wide, and under cross fire of artillery. No fords were used near the bridge, if any practical ones existed there . . . Regiments moved over the hill to the left and some from behind passed steadily over us through our ranks, some of the men seeming to prefer to join us for a while, but their officers preventing." The logjam Willcox's men experienced meant the division was unable to reach the western side of the Antietam until around 1400, letting another whole precious hour pass and allowing the Confederate troops at Sharpsburg a continued respite. When the division finally filed into position extending the *IX Corps* flank to the north astride the Lower Bridge Road, the entire force's line took the form of a convex arc, the bulge pointing west, extending from Snavely's Ford to north of the Lower Bridge Road.

The *IX Corps'* inability to quickly move forward on the offensive understandably infuriated the already exasperated McClellan. The army commander responded by sending another of his staff officers, Colonel Thomas M. Key to press his old friend Burnside to take some aggressive action. Key took with him a secret imperative from the *Army of the Potomac's* commander, a message to relieve Burnside with Major General George W. Morell, a *V Corps*

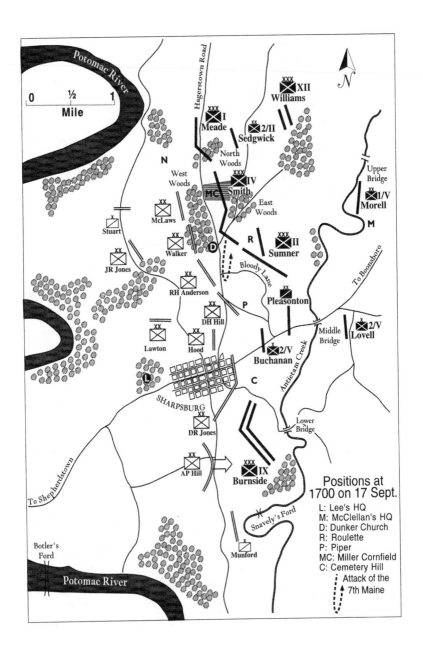

division commander, if the *IX Corps* failed to act according to McClellan's wishes. Despite his superior's call for urgency, Burnside failed to take a stronger hand in pressing his soldiers up against Sharpsburg, though he did cross to the western side of the Antietam to urge on his men and consult with his subordinates there. Another hour passed into oblivion as the *IX Corps* prepared itself for the task ahead.

The lull in major battlefield action did not mean that soldiers on both sides remained idle. As ever in such contests, pickets exchanged shots in the no-man's-land between the waiting lines of the contending forces while cannoneers took aim at distant targets that proved attractive. The Confederate artillery was particularly active and proved especially effective during these moments, making the *IX Corps'* wait agonizing and brutal, even in spite of a formidable Federal counterbattery fire. Now benefitting from their superior position on the high ground outside of Sharpsburg, the Federals' position unfolded beneath them like an amphitheater, leaving few places they could not drop their deadly carriage of shells and balls. All in all, Jones's Division had almost 40 guns trained on the Union position. The hail of iron the Confederate guns belched forth sent the *IX Corps* Yankees seeking cover, by either hugging the ground, or finding some other means to escape the near continuous deadly rain that filled the air. The unfortunate few who failed in this desperate enterprise only helped to increase their respective commands' tally of dead and wounded.

Union accounts of this furious cannonade are nearly unanimous in their descriptions of its ferocity. General Cox remembered the fire in his report ". . . the enemy kept up an incessant cannonade, and, having the exact range of the valley and the ravines, his shells came in very fast, annoying us a good deal and causing numerous casualties, notwithstanding the men were kept lying on the ground near the crests of the hill while changes in the line and the partially new formation after the arrival of Willcox's division were being made." Colonel Benjamin Christ's *1st*

Brigade had an especially tough time during the bombardment since Confederate artillery batteries on its front and left subjected the unit to a terrific crossfire. B. F. Blakeslee of the *16th Connecticut* recalled the fire when his unit assailed the ridge beyond the bridge: "By this time the rebel batteries were all roaring. They opened on us in all their fury. The air was filled with bullets and fiendish missiles. Hundreds [an exaggeration, but proof of the extent of which Federals suffered] of cannon were now aimed at us; grape and cannister, marbles and railroad iron were showered down like rain." The *48th Pennsylvania's* Oliver Bosbyshell remembered vividly being under the barrage of shot and shell from Confederate guns and the awful injuries it caused: "My! That was a hot place! Thermometer way up above the nineties. Whiz! whip! chung! The bullets came pelting into the ranks. With a bang and a sputter along came that destructive old shell, which filled Douty's eyes with dirt, bruised his shoulder, tore off Sergeant Seward's left and left Sergeant Trainer minus one arm, as it drove the ramrod he was just replacing into poor Cullen's breast. Cullen jumped to his feet, tore open his shirt to show his captain the wound, and then dropped dead at Winlack's feet."

Confederate gunners were especially quick to take aim whenever Federal troops presented themselves as targets. The commander of the *46th New York*, Lieutenant Colonel Gerhardt, experienced this deadly swiftness when his command went into position. His regiment, part of Welsh's brigade in Willcox's division, fell under the aim of Confederate cannon after they had crossed the bridge and ascended a hill left of the Lower Bridge Road. The colonel wrote in his report to Colonel Welsh that "[the regiment] came under a galling fire of shot and shell as soon as it was in sight of a battery posted by the enemy on a hill to our right."

The fierceness of the Confederate barrage and infantry fire belied the scant ranks of infantry Jones had on hand to field Burnside's eventual advance. The only reinforcements they had received this far were the survivors of the regiments that had fought at the Lower Bridge. The men from 2nd and 20th Georgia had retreated southwest from the bridge to the 40-Acre Cornfield and were later joined by less than 125 men of the 50th Georgia fleeing Rodman's advance from Snavely's Ford. These took position in the western vicinity of the 40-Acre Cornfield. Together, they now formed an advanced position on the far right wing of Jones's position and the Army of Northern Virginia.

A more sizable contingent of reinforcements was on the way from another direction. At 0630, Major General A. P. Hill had received orders from Lee to have his division make the 17-mile march from Harper's Ferry to the Confederate position at Sharpsburg. In a stark contrast with the *IX Corps'* sluggishness, Hill's Light Division obeyed Lee's command with astonishing speed. An hour after receiving the order Hill's brigades, save one, were on the move. At 1430, Hill, dressed in his red battle shirt, reported to Lee's headquarter's west of town with word that his troops were closing in on the threatened Confederate right flank.   The relieved General Lee supposedly welcomed the division commander with the words, "General Hill, I was never before so glad to see you, you are badly needed, put your force in on the right as fast as they come up." With every moment the *IX Corps'* delayed renewal of its attack, Hill's men were allowed to come closer and closer to the Sharpsburg battlefield and play a part in the day's course of events.

Around 1500, five hours after the Federals had begun to move against Confederate positions across the bridge and two hours after the bridge had been taken, Burnside ordered the *IX Corps*, through Cox, to have its ranks advance forward again and take Sharpsburg and the heights south of the town. All the corps' divisions save Sturgis's, which would remain on the ridge before the Lower Bridge, were to advance. Willcox's brigades were to move on the right toward Sharpsburg itself which lay only a mile away from their starting position. Rodman's units were supposed to advance in the same direction, pitching into the enemy forces in front of them and once these were driven away, move to the right en echelon on Willcox's left. Both divisions could count on artillery support by receiving covering fire from the Federal batteries on hand.

Shortly after 1515, the *IX Corps* was finally on the move again, nearly three divisions heading west. Beyond the undulating terrain they had to cross was D. R. Jones's thin line of infantry supported by artillery, waiting to greet them.

CHAPTER 9

ATTACK OF CHRIST'S BRIGADE, WILLCOX'S DIVISION

AROUND MIDAFTERNOON, Brigadier General Orlando Will-cox's two brigades, the 1st under Colonel Benjamin C. Christ and the 2nd under Colonel Thomas Welsh, swept northeast toward Sharpsburg, beginning their march on either side of the Lower Bridge Road near the Antietam Creek. Though the reserve of the IX Corps and the freshest troops Burnside could now field, Willcox's advance turned out to be fitful, slow, and irresolute.

Besides the Confederates of Jones's Division, the primary impediment Willcox's brigades faced on their drive was the nature of the terrain before them. This inconvenienced their march while lending the enemy several advantages. Both the division's brigades found their ability to keep an even pace with one another impeded by uneven heights on either side of the ravine through which the Lower Bridge Road ran. Moreover, any progress over this rolling country was made all the more difficult by wood and stone fences bordering fields and lanes, lying like hurdles for the advancing ranks. But if the ground made an advance difficult, it was well-suited for Confederate sharpshooters to harass their opponents. These troops found hiding places and covered positions to undertake their deadly work, hiding behind fences and among the haystacks, orchards, and cornfields. The ground also proved beneficial to Confederate artillerists, providing them with a commanding line of fire from their high ground on Cemetery Hill east of Sharpsburg, down

Modern-day view from Cemetery Hill out toward Lower Bridge Road. Rebel artillery units used this commanding line of fire to harass the Union drive.

the Lower Bridge Road nearly all the way to the Antietam Creek.

Commanding the right of the Willcox's advance was Benjamin C. Christ, a Pennsylvanian who had held high rank in the *5th Pennsylvania* regiment as its lieutenant colonel, and the *50th Pennsylvania* as its colonel, before he was plucked for more distinguished command assignments. Christ had a fine collection of regiments to rely upon in the coming work, most veterans of Sherman's and Hunter's battles on the South Carolina coast: the *79th New York*, the *28th Massachusetts,* and the *50th Pennsylvania.* New to the brigade and battle was the *17th Michigan.* Christ's regiments were to advance across the plowed ground, stubble fields, and pasture land of the Sherrick Farm, north of the Lower Bridge Road. Christ's brigade moved forward to assail this ground with the *79th New York* in advance as skirmishers, the *17th Michigan* on the left, the *28th Massachusetts* in center, and the *50th Pennsylvania* on the right.

Christ's men made a stalwart advance, encountering cannon fire from the several Confederate batteries perched upon Cemetery Hill. The Federals also encountered a smattering of rifle fire southeast of the hill from some Confederates orphaned from Hood's Division.

Christ's primary opposition though was Richard Garnett's brigade of the 8th, 18th, 19th, 28th, and 56th Virginia regiments, combined bearing the name of its currently inactive commander Brigadier General George Edward Pickett, who had led the brigade through some of the great battles on the Peninsula before he was wounded at Gaines' Mill. To greet the advancing blue-clad ranks, Garnett had thrown out the 56th Virginia as skirmishers to protect the artillery stationed near his position that were coming under fire. Garnett then advanced the rest of the men of his brigade into the corn to meet the enemy's attack. He later wrote in the report of his defense, "I moved my command some distance to the front in the standing corn (as many of my guns were short range), in order that they could produce more effect, and opened fire. At this time, I do not think my effective force could have exceeded 200 men, yet these, with two rifled pieces, most gallantly and skillfully served, under the command of Captain Moody, and superintended by Colonel Lee, checked and held at bay a force of the enemy many times our number." Garnett downplayed his numbers though not by much. He may have had 240 men on hand and was backed up by many more cannon on Cemetery Hill. Still his forces were minor compared to those Christ threw against him. Moreover, the Virginian had another potential adversary to worry about when Federal forces advancing over the middle bridge began probing in his direction.

Division commander Willcox proved exuberant about Christ's performance before Garnett's defense. He related in his report that, despite a severe enemy cannonade, the brigade's advance, supported by artillery, was a successful one, involving the ejection of the Confederate forces that opposed him from the field.

Christ himself was less sanguine about the suffering his command endured while covering the ground before Sharpsburg. Christ claimed his troops were faced by a battery "heavily" supported by infantry in the rear of a cornfield north of the Lower Bridge Road who punished his ranks as they closed on Sharpsburg from the southwest. Worse still, the brigade was not able to easily sweep forward to deal with these forces. After Christ's brigade scattered Colonel McMaster's detachments before them, the unit reached the crest of the hill before the Sherrick Farm Lane, where his men were about 350 yards distant from the Confederate battery in front. There it was discovered that the pace of Christ's partner in Willcox's attack, Welsh's brigade, was lagging on its advance south of the Lower Bridge Road. Uncomfortable with pressing on against a combined infantry and artillery force in his front and

A present-day photo of the ground over which Willcox's division passed. To the left behind the trees is a statue of Benjamin Christ.

annoying blasts of artillery enfilading his left flank, Christ had his troops pause on the high ground. There was little cover available for the unfortunate Federals in this position, who had been suffering from an artillery crossfire since their arrival on the field west of the Antietam. Their ranks, exposed on the hill, continued to endure the punishing infantry fusillades and artillery shelling in their front and flank while they awaited the renewal of their advance.

Finally, when Welsh had come up, Christ was able to get his troops on the move again against the enemy that had been harassing them. The historian of the *79th New York* recounted his unit's part in the drive: "Owing to the deadly fire, part of our supporting column was obliged to fall back, but the *2nd U.S. Regulars* succeeded in joining us and together we held the line, while the right wing of the Highlanders advanced still further, and did some execution against the enemy's gunners." The regulars referred to were part of Captain John S. Poland's *10th* and *11th U.S. Regiments,* part of Major General Fitz John Porter's *V Corps* operating in the vicinity of the Middle Bridge. Poland's men were protecting some batteries which had been sent across the Middle Bridge up toward Sharpsburg and had advanced his own command west reaching a point where the Sherrick Farm Lane joins the Boonsboro Pike where they were able to offer Christ's men some assistance.

Also on the right of Christ's brigade was the *50th Pennsylvania.* The historian of the regiment, Lewis Crater, a first lieutenant with the regiment's *Company F,* thought his unit's advance against the Confederates was a brief one. Even though the regiment, exhausted from picket duty the night before the battle, participated in the action with the greatest "alacrity and enthusiasm, charging upon and driving the enemy from his position." Still, the regiment endured no small loss with some 57 men falling killed and wounded. Among these was the captain of Company K, James Ingham, who fell directing the fire of his troops, his last words being, "Attention, Company! Aim, Fire!"

On the left, the *17th Michigan* tussled with some of

Colonel F. W. McMaster's troops in an orchard east of the Sherrick Farm. McMaster's troops had retired here from their initial position southeast of Cemetery Hill after being forced to retreat by Christ's advance. Matters were made all the worse for the novice Michigan troops when the Confederates were joined by Jenkins's Brigade under Lieutenant Colonel Joseph Walker. Walker's first position had been in support of the batteries on the outskirts of town, but he advanced troops into the orchard west of the Sherrick farm buildings to fend off Christ's advancing line. It wasn't until help arrived from Welsh's brigade that the annoyance caused by these forces was finally cleared.

By now, the Southerners facing Christ had begun to suffer a toll from the afternoon engagement as well. The Confederate gunners on Cemetery Hill had taken casualties from Federal counterbattery fire and their ammunition supplies began to dwindle due to their activity throughout the day. Christ reported he was finally able to drive away the Confederate gunners and Garnett's infantry opposing him east of Sharpsburg after his brigade renewed the offensive.

Though eventually driven from the field, Garnett's regiments had managed to keep up a strong enough fire to at least delay the outcome. Garnett now had his men fall back through Sharpsburg reporting later of his retreat, ". . . I discovered that the Federals had turned our extreme right, which began to give way, and a number of the Yankee flags appeared on the hill in the rear of the town and not far from our only avenue of escape. I ordered the brigade to fall back, deeming it in imminent danger of being surrounded and captured, as it would have been impossible for it to have held its position without the support of the troops on the right. There being some delay in withdrawing Moody's section of artillery, I take pleasure in saying I saw Major Campbell halt and face his men about, to await its removal . . ."

Once in Sharpsburg, Garnett found a scene of confusion, a disorganized mass of his comrades refugees from the great conflagration that had taken place around the town throughout the day: "The main street of the town was commanded by the Federal artillery. My troops, therefore, passed, for the most part, to the north of the town along the cross streets. In this direction I found troops scattered in squads from various parts of the army, so that it was impossible to distinguish men of the different commands."

The Federals had driven the Confederates from ground east of Sharpsburg and Cemetery Hill. But on the outskirts of the enemy's chaos within the town, Christ proved too wary to press his advantage into the town. He recounted in his report how he cautiously halted his troops outside of Sharpsburg rather than press forward in pursuit: "I did not deem it prudent to advance after his artillery had retired, for the reason that the woods were lined with his sharpshooters, and I would only have exposed my command to their fire without gaining anything. I retired my charging party to my line of battle, and maintained my position until ordered to take another farther down and near the bridge, where the men slept on their arms for the night." This ability to push the Confederate line from the field, yet fail to push on in the face of their retreat was a story that would be repeated throughout the day.

CHAPTER 10

The Attack of Welsh's Brigade, Willcox's Division

Garnett's defeat was only one instance of the *IX Corps'* ability to brush aside segments of D. R. Jones's understrength division. Christ's fellow commander Welsh was to enjoy like success.

Welsh appeared to have more fighting mettle than his co-commander in Willcox's advance. Welsh's troops would cover the ground immediately south of the Lower Bridge Road. Before them the ground was mostly open, being pastureland, plowed fields, or stubble that rose and fell into Otto Farm ravine before rising steeply toward the high ground of the Harper's Ferry Road as it entered Sharpsburg. Leading Welsh's advance was the *100th Pennsylvania* acting as skirmishers, followed by the *45th Pennsylvania* on the right, the *46th New York* in the center, and the *8th Michigan* on the left. These troops began their advance from a position to the left of the Lower Bridge Road east of the Otto Farm.

Welsh's troops encountered much interference on their right. After driving off members of the 15th South Carolina from Drayton's Brigade, serving as skirmishers just north of the Otto Farm buildings, the Yankee's encountered a Confederate strongpoint across the Lower Bridge Road in the orchard where McMaster's men and South Carolinians, joined by regiments from Jenkins's Brigade, were holding up. As Colonel McMaster told of the action in his official report, he was able to hold back the Federals for quite a while in his new position: "About 3 p.m. a brigade of the

97

enemy flanked my command on the right, and, after firing a few moments, the Holcombe Legion and a few of the Seventeenth Regiment, in spite of my efforts, broke and ran. I then ordered the remainder of my command to retire to an apple orchard, about 200 yards in rear, with 40 or 50 men, made up mostly of my regiment and a few Georgians and Palmetto Sharpshooters, I fought the enemy for half an hour or more."

To help eject the Confederates and provide some artillery support at close quarters, Lieutenant John N. Coffin brought two guns of his four-gun section of the *8th Massachusetts Artillery* to help out with the contest. His guns went into position on the Otto Farm Lane, southeast of the orchard where McMaster and Walker's forces were. From his new position, Coffin alternated between targets northeast of him, blasting away at the Jenkins's Brigade and McMasters's troops, the telling shots at close range eventually driving most of the men off, and the Confederate artillery on Cemetery Hill.

However, the Confederate opposition had not yet departed the field entirely, finding another strong position to contest the Federal advance. According to McMaster, after his men had been cleared of the orchard north of the Sherrick farm they retreated south a short distance to the stone house where they continued to fight it out with the soldiers of Welsh's right, primarily the *100th Pennsylvania* and *45th Pennsylvania*. The battle became a bitter firefight with the Federals finally dislodging the Confederates from their strongholds, taking prisoners, and sending the rest running for safety, the cost of the victory being a number of casualties. After battling the Federals McMaster retreated to the high ground east of Sharpsburg, facing Welsh's advancing ranks. There he maintained his position in the face of the oncoming onslaught.

Welsh continued his march to the limits of Sharpsburg, but finding his brigade had gone too far in advance of the forces on both flanks in approaching Sharpsburg from the south, he decided the situation dictated caution and called

A present-day photo of the stone house and mill where Welsh's troops fought a bitter firefight against the Confederates.

a halt in the orchard just south of Sharpsburg. Though the colonel did not wish to move farther, his men were eager to continue the offensive: "I had great difficulty in restraining the ardor of my troops, who seemed anxious to charge through the town and capture the batteries beyond." On his right were Walker's tenacious troops of Jenkins's Brigade that had not yet quit the field. After Welsh's and Christ's men forced his troops out of the orchard, they headed northeast where they found a stone wall outside of town behind which they adopted a new position facing south.

Crook's *Kanawha* brigade was also active in its supporting role during Welsh's assault. With the *28th* and *36th Ohio* regiments in the advance, it had participated in the charge through a ravine near the Otto Farm against Drayton's 15th South Carolina. The Ohioans came under some artillery fire while passing through the ravine, shelling which took the life of the Colonel Melvin Clarke, the *36th*'s commander.

Willcox's division had successfully driven back or driven off much of the Confederate force of Jenkins's and Garnett's brigades. In his official report, the jubilant commander expressed his satisfaction in his division's progress, "Our musket ammunition was now exhausted. We had carried the heights of Sharpsburg, and rested partly in the town and partly on the hills. The enemy kept up a desultory fire along our line, but a respectful distance . . . " Yet, due to either lack of ammunition or will, the general was unable to press his advantage in numbers any further into the Confederate rear. Meanwhile, further success was obtained by the *IX Corps* arms to the left of Willcox's assault, where Fairchild's Brigade of Rodman's division was engaged.

CHAPTER 11

ATTACK OF FAIRCHILD'S BRIGADE, RODMAN'S DIVISION

THE DRIVE OF WILLCOX'S BRIGADES was unexceptional in its advance or in its results. Sheer mass of manpower had been employed to drive off a weaker foe though Jenkins's brigade tenuously hung on outside Sharpsburg, disputing the Federal gains with some angry, stubborn fire. The force operating on Willcox's left achieved a more decisive result, Colonel Harrison S. Fairchild's *1st Brigade* of Rodman's division, composed of the *9th New York, 89th New York,* and *103rd New York.* This command's advance marked the most impressive charge in this sector of the field if not the entire battle of Antietam.

For the most part, the ground over which Fairchild's New Yorkers would have to advance was clear, bereft of the strong points and hiding places that benefitted the Confederates facing Willcox's advance, the primary obstructions being lines of farm fences dividing fields into awkward rectangles or distended polygons. The major difficulty faced by Fairchild's New Yorkers was scrambling up and down the steep slopes that lay before them. Once past the Otto Farm Lane, the ground descended sharply into the Otto Farm ravine, across which a plowed field lay. A short distance west of the ravine the ground dipped again, dropping slightly into another shallower trough, just before ascending into a high plateau, south of Sharpsburg and just east of the Harper's Ferry Road. This hill was destined to be the point at which Fairchild's New Yorker's would clash with Jones's line. The path toward that point was fraught with danger. While the depressions along the way would offer the New Yorkers some cover during their charge, once on the crests the infantry would be an open target for Confederate gunners.

Fairchild's troops would make their charge with the *89th New York* on the left, flanked by the *103rd New York* on its right, and then the *9th New York* on the far right, reaching out for Welsh's brigade. Waiting for the New Yorkers were the two brigades of Drayton and Kemper.

Kemper's thin regiments were spread out along the line east of the Harper's Ferry Road. When they took their position on the plateau's crest, the 11th Virginia was immediately on Drayton's right, close to the stone fence's junction with the rail fence. To the right was the 1st Virginia and then the 17th Virginia. The 7th and 24th Virginia, posted farther south down the road, did not play a part in withstanding Fairchild's attack. On the far right of the Confederate position was another of Kemper's regiments, the 17th Virginia under Colonel Montgomery Corse, which was a mere skeleton of its former strength. Only around 50 of the

A present-day look at the heights beyond the Otto Farm ravine where Jones's brigade awaited the Federal advance.

more than 800 men that had joined the regiment remained to fight on the Antietam battlefield.

For most of the day, the 17th Virginia listened with awe to the distant echoes of the battle's mighty confrontations taking place to the north, but now the 17th Virginia would take on hundreds of Federals in Fairchild's advancing brigade.

The command for Fairchild's regiments to advance came from General Rodman himself after he had inspected the Confederate position from afar. First he directed each of the brigade's regiments to send forth a detachment of skirmishers. After Rodman saw Willcox's troops on the move to the north, the division commander ordered the rest of Fairchild's men forward. The historians in Hawkins's Zouave regiment recorded much of Fairchild's advance. When the *9th New York Zouaves* received the order to charge, M. J. Graham thought it must be a mistake. The idea of standing in the face of the considerable shot and shell being blasted from Confederate artillery at the time seemed absurd. The Zouave charge became a series of sprints and pauses as the nattily-dressed soldiers scrambled through the enemy fire and hit the ground for rest when cover could be found.

The first obstacle the Zouaves faced were the rail fences of the Otto Farm Lane which they pushed or scrambled over on the advance. Heading northwest the unit paused in the ravine there, taking cover momentarily from bursts of shrapnel sent by the enemy's cannon. Then, suddenly, the troops in Fairchild's regiments once more took to their feet, continuing their charge onward, driving away skirmishers of the 7th Virginia, coming to a halt before another slight depression, this one just before the main Confederate line.

On the other side of the field, the *9th New York* had been losing men steadily nearly ever since it had begun the charge. Even under its current cover, the enemy's artillery fire still took a toll. The commander of the *9th* ignored the danger, stomping up and down his line belting out words of encouragement to his men. Some of the *9th*'s soldiers looked back over the path of their advance and could see a long trail of bodies, some laying in brief rows as if they had been standing side by side when they were felled at the same time.

The Confederates were beginning to feel some pressure as well. Brown's and Reilly's guns harassed Fairchild's Zouaves as they advanced, an endeavor which proved increasing hazardous due to severe counterbattery fire. Brown's battery took several casualties, it's commander among them, and was forced to pull out. Private Hunter recalled Brown's withdrawal with great resentment, ". . . the battery with us limbered up and moved away, because, as they said, their ammunition was exhausted; but murmurs and curses loud and deep were heard from the brigade, who openly charged the battery was deserting them in the coming ordeal." Eventually joining Brown's withdrawal were Reilly's guns, pulling out as the New Yorkers closed on Jones's line. The Confederate infantry was not totally without artillery support however. Brown's pieces were soon replaced by McIntosh's Pee Dee artillery, a recent arrival from A. P. Hill's Light Division. Cannoneer J. L. Napier was with the battery as it rode onto the field just as Brown's guns were coming off the field. Sensing the situation before them was desperate, Napier called out to his commander, "Captain, see those men are leaving there, we had better not go in." McIntosh discounted the warning. Napier remembered his captain's reply, "I am ordered to go in there and go to fighting." There were only around 21 men with the battery at the time it went into action. It began by pelting Fairchild's oncoming troops with canister as soon as it went into position south of the 17th Virginia.

Finally, their pause over, Fairchild's men set off on the last series of steps toward Jones's position, but by now fully a third of their comrades had fallen. The survivors' orders were to press forward with bayonets fixed, fire a volley and then charge over the Confederate position. These final moments of Fairchild's charge were especially painful. Drayton's and Kemper's Confederates patiently allowed the advancing Yankee line to come within close range where they could unleash a killing fusillade with devastating effect. Drayton's troops rested their muzzles on the stone wall before them, while Kemper's men positioned their guns on the fence rails before them. When the *9th New York* swept upon Drayton's men, they suffered a blistering torrent of lead from the Confederates at a range of maybe 50 yards. Graham and scores of his comrades fell as casualties in the grueling blasts.

Some of Drayton's troops were captured, others were scattered into Sharpsburg or the Avey Orchard. Of all of the Confederate regiments, one, the 15th South Carolina under Colonel W. S. De Saussure, retreated from the front slowly and in order, forming, in the words of Major General Jones, "the nucleus on which the brigade rallied." To Drayton's right, Kemper had faired no better withstanding Fairchild's attack.

The *103rd New York* and *89th New York* pressed forward firing, their ranks lapping up against Kemper's weak com-

The gallant charge of the *9th New York Zouaves* as they came within sight of the town of Sharpsburg. They were turned back by a torrent of Confederate lead.

mands who must have watched wide-eyed at the huge host assembled against them. Either the *103rd* or *89th New York* regiments may have come into view of 1st Virginia's Dooley, who awaited their approach with some apprehension. Dooley and his comrades managed to only get off a volley before they made a break for the rear. The 1st Virginia was not the only command to crack. The retreat was taken up by the rest of the regiments in Kemper's brigade. Kemper's Brigade was overwhelmed and outflanked as soon as the Federal ranks surged forward over their line. Not all of Fairchild's men enjoyed palpable success. His center regiment, the *103rd New York* staggered to a halt under the enemy's musketry only 50 feet from their line behind the fence.

With Kemper's and Drayton's brigades sent fleeing to the rear, most of D. R. Jones's line had practically all but disintegrated. The division's splintered Confederate brigades fled west toward Harper's Ferry Road, at least those who were able to make an escape. Of Jones's brigades at Sharpsburg, only one, Jenkins's under Walker, was holding its position east of Sharpsburg, facing south and firing on the Federals in that direction, they had not yet been driven from the front line.

At the peak of its victory, Fairchild's brigade began to lose a semblance of order as a few over-enthusiastic Yankees decided to continue the charge on their own, following the retreating enemy as far as Sharpsburg itself. Commanders recalled most of the impetuous soldiers, eager to renew the offensive in a more organized manner as soon as support arrived. Officers with the *9th New York* had to threaten their men with revolvers to keep them from going too far ahead. One Zouave, in his unfortunate zeal, did manage to make his way into Sharpsburg only to meet his death there. His lifeless body was later recovered from one of the town's streets.

The cost of Fairchild's success had not come cheap. His brigade lost 455 of 940 men during the day, nearly half his strength, with heaviest casualties suffered by the *9th New*

York who lost 235 men or 63 percent of their number on their terrific advance. The *103rd New York* suffered the next highest number of casualties—117 men, slightly over half the command. The regiment with the least number of casualties was the *89th New York* with 103 men lost, almost 30 percent of its members.

Jones's division had been broken, the Confederate right flank was in desperate jeopardy and the *IX Corps* was finally close to being victorious. Yet with ultimate success at hand, it was to remain defiantly elusive. A Federal signal station on Elk Ridge flagged a message to General Burnside that was a warning sign of what was to come: "To General Burnside: Look out well on your left; the enemy are moving a strong force in that direction." It was A. P. Hill's division arriving from Harper's Ferry at this desperate hour and its brigades were preparing to launch a powerful counterattack, falling upon the brigade that comprised Rodman's left flank, Harland's *2nd Brigade*. The timely arrival of this force seemed more than fortuitous. As Longstreet later remarked, Lee had commanded Hill and his Light Division to join the Army of Northern Virginia and as if "by magic" they arrived on the field to deal with the "final crisis."

CHAPTER 12

REPULSE OF HARLAND'S BRIGADE, RODMAN'S DIVISION

As FORMIDABLE AS THE *IX CORPS'* ATTACK against Jones's position at Sharpsburg may have seemed, it contained a glaring Achilles Heel, a critical weakness toward which Hill's oncoming brigades were unknowingly headed. The corps' left flank had been entrusted to Colonel Edward Harland's brigade of New England regiments, the *8th* and *16th Connecticut* and *4th Rhode Island*. Of these regiments, the *8th Connecticut* and *4th Rhode Island* were fairly experienced, but the *16th Connecticut* was about as unprepared for the fight as soldiers could possibly be. Though the regiment's commander, Colonel Francis Beach, was a regular army officer, the rank and file of the *16th* were brand-new troops. Here, on the fields at Sharpsburg, their inexperience proved a fatal handicap as a cruel train of circumstances enshrouded them in a maelstrom of battlefield chaos at the worst possible time, in the worst possible place for themselves and for their corps.

The positioning of the *16th Connecticut* would not have been so detrimental save for a significant feature in the path of its advance. To the left and in-between the brigade and the Harper's Ferry Road was a huge, dense expanse of Indian corn, 40 acres in size, spread out over the trough of the Otto Farm ravine. Field fences demarcated its borders, mostly of wooden rails though the southwestern face was almost entirely a stone wall. This was not "The Cornfield" of the battle of Antietam's lore; that field was situated east of the Dunker Church, north of Sharpsburg, where Con-

The area that comprised the 40-Acre Cornfield can still be seen on a tour of the Antietam battlefield.

federates and Federals had been slaughtered earlier in the day. However, the corn rows before Harland's New Englanders were just as significant for it was here that the *IX Corps'* advance would suddenly become imperiled. It has since gone down in historical accounts with the rather conventional designation of "The 40-Acre Cornfield."

What made the 40-Acre Cornfield so dangerous was the obvious fact that the rows of corn obscured the line of sight of troops operating within its confines. Moreover, the cornfield was planted over the wide ravine cutting across the Otto Farm from north to south. In that cornfield and ravine, troops could hardly have any idea what was going on around them or know whether they were flanked by friendly troops or the foe. It was into this place that the rookies of the *16th Connecticut*, 760-men strong, would go and where Harland's brigade would begin to fall apart.

Another plot of corn that served as a scene for this part of the battle was just west of the 40-Acre Cornfield, roughly 700 yards south of Sharpsburg, 150 yards in length fronting the Harper's Ferry Road. Just north of this field was where McIntosh's guns had set up to harass Fairchild's advance.

110

This smaller field, known in some accounts as the "Narrow Cornfield" also came to obtain some dangerous significance for the Union advance.

At first, the corn rows appeared a boon to Harland's troops. Like most of their comrades across the field, Harland's regiments had been suffering barrages from Confederate cannon on the high ground south of Sharpsburg. The corn hid the brigade from enemy gunners' ready eyes, providing a needed respite from their cannonade. With this advantage in mind, the *16th Connecticut* and *4th Rhode Island* were advanced into the field to secure its cover. The *16th* was in the lead, moving into the corn and then filing down into the ravine where the regiment threw out skirmishers.

Once troops were within the 40-Acre Cornfield, the position became a menace. When Rodman ordered Harland's brigade to march west on the offensive, the *8th Connecticut*, on the force's right, received the command and dutifully headed in the appointed direction. The rest of the brigade in the 40-Acre Cornfield, the *16th Connecticut* and the *4th Rhode Island*, never received the initial order to move out and remained oblivious of the need to press on. The separation of one-third of his brigade from the remainder led Harland to ask Rodman if he should halt the *8th Connecticut* until the other regiments received their orders and moved up. Harland recounted that the general ordered him to continue while taking upon himself the task of bringing up the tardy regiments. Harland remained with the *8th Connecticut* as it continued its march, then heading northeast to join with Fairchild's left held by the *89th New York*.

The *8th Connecticut* swarmed northwest across the Otto Farm, assailing the high ground and passing in front of McIntosh's Pee Dee artillery that had stayed on the field after much of Jones's Division had been swept away. The artillerists spied the advancing ranks surge before them and punished the Yankees with destructive bursts of canister. Captain Charles L. Upham with the *8th Connecticut's*

Company K was detached to deal with cannoneers. They endured severe fire from the guns as they stormed forward. The Yankees were only thwarted momentarily. Soon they were coming on again, closing within 50 to 75 yards of the gunners. McIntosh's men increasingly began to suffer for their defiance when the Federals began returning fire of their own, shooting down several cannoneers and artillery horses. A hasty withdrawal now became the primary preoccupation of the remaining Pee Dee gunners.

Upham's force rejoined the *8th Connecticut* just as the unit found itself in a dangerously lonesome situation. They had reached the high ground's crest south of where Fairchild's men had been engaged. While they found the litter of battlefield carnage, the troops that were supposed to be on their right flank had moved off elsewhere, veering farther north to deal with the remnants of Jones's Division. At the same time, the rest of Harland's regiments had failed to make their appearance on the *8th Connecticut*'s left. The soldiers that could be seen from their position were Confed-

Troops in a battle amidst the cornfields of Sharpsburg. The high cornfields of September played strategic roles in the battle of Antietam.

erates, both in front of the regiment and now on its left flank as well.

Watching the progress of the *8th Connecticut* was one of Kemper's regiments stationed on the far right flank, the 113 men of the 7th Virginia under Captain Philip S. Ashby. Ashby's unit, stationed on the Confederate far right, had yet to be engaged. As of this moment, it had only watched Confederate skirmishers scatter an advance line of Union troops far away at the base of the hill before them. Captain Ashby, a veteran of the Mexican War, now gave his troops a grim "stand or die" order: "Men, we are to hold this position at all hazards. Not a man must leave his place. If need be, we will die together here in this road." The only friendly force on hand to assist them was a collection of Georgian soldiers to their right flank culled together by Henry Benning, the survivors of the defense of the Lower Bridge and Snavely's Ford, along with the recently arrived 15th Georgia, 17th Georgia, and five companies of the 11th Georgia. These newcomers had earlier been sent off pursuing Federals who had escaped capture at Harper's Ferry and, after giving up the chase, rejoined the rest of the Army of Northern Virginia after seizure of the Lower Bridge, its men exhausted after long marching.

Before the 7th Virginia could fire, ranks of Confederate troops passed before their front, members of the newly arrived Light Division of A. P. Hill. After getting information on the ground from D. R. Jones, Hill obeyed the directive he had received from Lee by sending in his brigades piecemeal as they arrived near the field, moving up from Boteler's Ford via the Sawmill Road, a route intersecting with the Harper's Ferry Road roughly three quarters of a mile south of Sharpsburg. Hill met his incoming troops at the Blackford Farm, just off the Sawmill Road before it merged with the Harper's Ferry Road and distributed his brigades to shore up the shattered Confederate right flank. The exact order of the arrival of the Light Division is not known. Two of his brigades, Pender's and Brockenbrough's, were sent to the extreme right, in Hill's words,

A. P. Hill and his Confederate troops arrived at the battle at just the strategic moment when they were able to turn back the Union advance and regain most of the ground lost throughout the day.

"looking to a road which crossed the Antietam near its mouth." Three other brigades, Archer's, Branch's, and Gregg's, were sent to assist his fellow division commander's line which had since collapsed. Many in these oncoming ranks sported Federal blue uniforms and even carried Union colors, all of these being part of the plunder captured at Harper's Ferry.

Both Gregg's and Branch's brigades came to operate on positions that would take them against the Federal far left flank. Gregg's Brigade would take the leading role in the coming attack. This force was commanded by Brigadier General Maxcy Gregg and composed of the 1st, 12th, 13th, and 14th South Carolina regiments along with the 1st South Carolina Rifles.

Gregg's line was formed with the 13th South Carolina on the left, the 12th in the center, and the 1st on the right. The 1st South Carolina Rifles were retained as a reserve. Gregg's regiments then headed into the 40-Acre Cornfield from the southwest, bearing down on the hapless Federal regiments there, sweeping aside the Yankee skirmishers before them. Indeed, Gregg's troops were going in where they were most needed and where they could deliver a telling blow with great effect.

The Federals were not completely incognizant of the danger posed by Gregg's Brigade. Colonel Harland himself spied the enemy forces moving toward the endangered left flank of his lagging regiments in the cornfield. Desperately, the colonel galloped off to warn his men only to have his horse fall injured from the storm of iron and lead flying about the field. Harland had not been alone in his fear for the left flank. Rodman too had perceived the threat and ordered the Connecticut and Rhode Island regiments to change their front and face the enemy forces advancing against their left. Shortly after doing so, the officer was shot from his horse by a Rebel bullet and fell with a mortal wound. General Rodman's loss now left the beleaguered Colonel Harland in command of the division. Harland, though, was presently concerned solely with his own brigade.

The present-day intersection of Sawmill Road with Harper's Ferry Road where A. P. Hill's Light Division moved up into the battle at the 40-Acre Cornfield.

Harland's two regiments in the cornfield were coming under increasing jeopardy though their Confederate opposition experienced difficulty in launching their attack. Gregg's regimental commanders had different opinions as to what was expected of them. On Gregg's left, Colonel O. E. Edwards kept his 13th South Carolina in a defensive posture at the stone wall on the cornfield's southwestern face, while Colonel Dixon Barnes's 12th South Carolina and Colonel D. H. Hamilton's 1st South Carolina pressed forward to the northeast. The South Carolinians came to overlook the *16th Connecticut* in the cornfield at the base of the Otto Farm ravine. With a fine advantage in position, they proceeded to pepper the Yankees below with musketry.

Suddenly, the *16th* found itself under a rain of enemy bullets. Harland finally reached the cornfield at the time this storm broke. He found the Connecticut regiment under threat, but also in a very opportune position. The *16th*'s regimental commanders had evidently received Rodman's order's to face the unit toward the left. When the *16th* was struck, it had become nearly parallel to and alongside Gregg's left flank. Harland then strove to have the regiment turn to enfilade the enemy line. While veterans might have undertaken the required movements in time, the Connecticut soldiers were far too inexperienced and only slowly began to turn toward the Confederate right flank.

The Connecticut troops were also getting the benefit of some reinforcements when their comrades from the *4th Rhode Island* advanced to their left. While the 247 men of the *4th* brought some extra firepower, they also added some significant disorganization to the line in the ravine. The Connecticut troops were already unnerved by the enemy's fire and the complex movements they were trying to undertake. Their numbers were bunching to the left where they jumbled the Rhode Islanders' line, already disorganized from its own march through the corn. To make matters worse for the *4th Rhode Island*, when its commanders saw the Confederates, they spotted the Stars and Stripes flying from the enemy's ranks—some of the colors that the Southerners had captured at Harper's Ferry and were putting to their own use during the battle. The regiment's commander, Colonel William Steere, feared he might be firing on friends and tried to sort out the confusing situation by determining the nature of the troops before him.

Once the nature of the troops was revealed, Colonel Steere then sought to launch an attack against the enemy. As Lieutenant Colonel Curtis recounted, an officer was sent to the *16th Connecticut* for aid in the assault, but the disorientation in the cornfield was just too great to put together any coordinated effort, ". . . Colonel Steere sent me to the Sixteenth Connecticut to see if they would support us in a charge up the hill, but the corn being very thick and high, I could find no one to whom to apply. I returned to tell the colonel that we must depend on ourselves. He then sent me to the rear for support."

At the moment, the Yankees' situation was serious but not yet hopeless. The *16th Connecticut* and *4th Rhode Island* still had support to rely upon in the form of Colonel Hugh Ewing's *Kanawha Division* brigade. Despite the confusion and handicaps the New England regiments endured in the cornfield, they might have held until the Ohioans arrived save for a single event that cast all their sacrifices into oblivion. Gregg was able to get his much smaller reserve, the 1st South Carolina Rifles under Lieutenant Colonel James Perrin, into the action first and almost exactly where it would have the desired effect. This unit went in on the right of the 1st South Carolina from whence they found their way to the Rhode Islanders' left flank. The South Carolinian's poured blast after destructive blast into the already confused Federal ranks.

The shots did more than take down casualties, they toppled the Federal troops' resolve. Finally broken, their numbers went streaming for the rear. The *16th Connecticut* actually had tried to rally in spite of its desperate position, losing a series of senior officers and several men in the attempt. The embattled and beleaguered *16th Connecticut* could prove no match for Gregg's South Carolinians under such circumstances and they utterly collapsed. Caldwell later said the retreat of the Connecticut troops made them even more vulnerable to his brigade's fire: "And when the enemy retreated they had to pass through open ground, which enabled us to kill large numbers of them. But our object was entirely defensive. It was enough, fully enough for this division to save the right flank of the army." The Rhode Islanders joined their Connecticut comrades in streaming for their rear. A try was made to rally the troops, an effort that went for naught after Colonel Steere was wounded in the thigh shortly after giving the order to retreat.

Off to the northwest, the final regiment of Harland's brigade was making a stand of its own. The *8th Connecticut* was on the high ground east of the Harper's Ferry Road and north of the Narrow Cornfield nervously watching a collection of Confederate forces massing on its left flank and in its front. Almost on the very left flank were elements of the formidable brigade of Brigadier General L. O'Brien Branch. Branch's brigade of the 7th, 18th, 28th, 33rd, and 37th North Carolina regiments had come on the field up the Sawmill Road until shelling from Federal artillery forced it to make a detour south almost mimicking the path of Gregg's Brigade. The brigade's lead regiments, the 7th and 37th North Carolina, passed over the Harper's Ferry Road heading east when the *8th Connecticut* caught its attention and it headed north toward the lone Yankee regiment. The North Carolinians came within 300 yards of the *8th Connecticut* forcing it to refuse its left to meet the attack.

Southwest of the Yankee regiment, north of the North Carolinians, was another force composed of Toombs's and Benning's ubiquitous Georgians. These had initially been west of the 40-Acre Cornfield until relieved by Gregg's Brigade. They had been brought forward to face the Connecticut troops by an indefatigable aide of Toombs, Captain J. L. Troup. Troup had urged Benning's men back into action farther north after most of Jones's Division had been driven from the field. Benning's men went back into the fighting by moving into the northwest corner of the Narrow Cornfield where they spotted McIntosh's abandoned artillery pieces and the *8th Connecticut* re-forming just a short distance beyond them. General Benning cunningly organized his troops to unleash some musketry against the Connecticut troops while concealing his rank's meager numbers.

In front of the *8th Connecticut* were the remnants of Kemper's and Drayton's brigades that had been organized by Toombs in the Harper's Ferry Road. The Confederate troops also had some artillery support on hand in the form of Richardson's battery. The combined forces were too much for a single unsupported regiment to bear.

Despite the ferocity of the forces Toombs and his comrades were directing against them, the *8th Connecticut* desperately attempted to resist. As proof the fight was going to be a tough one the regimental commander, Lieutenant Colonel Hiram Appleman, ordered the color-bearer not to desert the unit's banners. Protecting the flags before the oncoming sheet of bullets soon proved to be a hazardous occupation. The enemy fire began to take its toll on the colorguard who fell away one by one. Still, the *8th* had a ready supply of volunteers to hold the flags high in spite of the mounting cost in life. One such individual was Private Charles H. Walker who leapt forward to seize the flag, planting it in the ground and waving it defiantly against the enemy. Men continued to fall from the ranks, including Lieutenant Marvin Wait who remained in the thick of combat even though wounded in his right arm. Taking his sword in his left hand, Wait raised it high in the air to exhort on his men. His steadfastness proved his downfall as his body was riddled with enemy bullets and fell to the ground. On the Confederate side of the action, Benning's troops maintained a fierce sniping fire that enabled his men to recover McIntosh's abandoned pieces.

After Lieutenant Colonel Appleman was wounded and carried from the fighting, Major John E. Ward found himself in command. Ward wrote of the growing ferocity of the encounter, "The fire from artillery and musketry was very severe, the regiment receiving fire in front and on both flanks." Colonel Harland wrote of the regiment's desperate stand, "The Eighth Regiment Connecticut Volunteers, which had held their position until this time, now, by order of Major Ward, commanding, moved more to the right, where they were sheltered in a measure from the fire in front, and changed front, so as to reply to the enemy on the left. After a few rounds, as most of the men were out of ammunition, the order was given to fall back." The *8th Connecticut* took up the retreat, Private Walker bringing the National colors to safety. All in all, the regiment lost over half of its 350 men in the fighting. According to Colonel Harland, the *2nd Brigade* of Rodman's division was almost entirely spent. "At the bridge, I collected the shattered remnants of the brigade, in the hopes of making a stand, but, owing to the large loss of officers and the failure of ammunition, it was impossible to render the men of any material service."

With the disintegration of Harland's brigade, the initiative changed hands and the roles of both sides changed. The *IX Corps* would go from the offensive to the defensive while A. P. Hill and Toombs's men strove to regain the ground that had been thus far lost.

CHAPTER 13

STAND OF EWING'S BRIGADE, KANAWHA DIVISION

AFTER THE 8TH CONNECTICUT'S WITHDRAWAL in front of near insurmountable odds, Toombs continued his general advance. The prospect must have been daunting despite the movement's initial success. As implausible as it might seem, Toombs's collection of troops was about to retake much ground lost east of the Harper's Ferry Road, once and for all shutting down offensive capability of the much stronger IX Corps that had routed the Confederate ranks just moments before.

Private John E. Dooley and his comrades from Jones's division did not make their advance alone. Archer's brigade of A. P. Hill's Division, containing some 400 men, had since arrived on the field. They went into position to the right of where Toombs was organizing remnants of Jones's Division along the Harper's Ferry Road with part of it situated behind the Narrow Cornfield.

The brigade of Brigadier General James J. Archer, composed of the 19th Georgia and 1st, 7th, and 14th Tennessee regiments, formed a line along the plank fence parallel to Harper's Ferry Road but then endured an uncomfortable pause. But if waiting for the orders to move was uncomfortable, so was Archer's initial advance. It sputtered to a start from its position behind the Narrow Cornfield when someone suddenly called out "Fall Back!" Mistaking the voice for Archer's, part of the command complied with the order and the brigade had to be re-formed before it could move forward. When Archer's Brigade finally did press ahead from its Harper's Ferry Road position, it pressed through the Narrow Cornfield and headed for the northwestern corner of the 40-Acre Cornfield where it was bounded by a stone wall.

As the *IX Corps'* assaulting line withered away before the combined attacks of A. P. Hill's and D. R. Jones's brigades, stemming the now victorious Confederate tide fell to the only force Burnside had available that had yet to be severely engaged, Colonel Hugh Ewing's Ohioan *1st Brigade* of the *Kanawha Division*. This force, with the *12th Ohio* regiment taking the left flank joined by the *30th* and *23rd Ohio* on the right, advanced to replace Harland's vanquished command and shore up the deteriorating *IX Corps* left flank in the 40-Acre Cornfield's vicinity. Even the influx of these fresh troops into the tumultuous battle proved unable to block the seemingly near inexorable advance of the Confederate ranks.

Ewing now faced a formidable task on the fields at Sharpsburg. His lone brigade would have to fend off Gregg's Brigade on his left in the 40-Acre Cornfield as well as Archer's Brigade, Branch's North Carolina brigade, and the remainder of Jones's Division under Toombs's advancing in his front. His troops may have been too skittish by the day's events to succeed in this task, a point noted by the wounded Lieutenant Graham from the *9th New York*. Graham remembered passing a cowering brigade of Ohioans as he was carried to the rear, possibly Ewing's troops. The Ohioans' apprehension was understandable. The way the battle had turned, they were not going in to battle to insure a victory, but to forestall a defeat. Against them may have been a combined total of 2,000 Confederate troops.

The *12th Ohio* had the crucial role in Ewing's brigade's upcoming part in the battle—dispatching Confederate troops flanking the brigade in the 40-Acre Cornfield. To do this, the regiment was to take a position at a right angle to the rest of the brigade which was facing west, and then push south, clearing the enemy away. The regiment enjoyed some initial success when it fired into the 40-Acre

Cornfield's eastern face, scattering some South Carolinians of Gregg's Brigade. The regiment then advanced into the cornfield's northeastern corner only to find a whirlpool of bullets and shells hurled in their direction from both friend and foe. Confederate gunners from the batteries being massed on the high ground along the Harper's Ferry Road made the *12th* a target for their volleys of spherical case and shell. Adding to this bombardment was a clattering small-arms fire coming from the tenacious South Carolinians hundreds of yards off to the southwest. A Union artillery battery attempting to reply to its Confederate counterparts did not help matters when it placed some of its shots in the Ohioans ranks. Making the situation all the more extreme was a smattering of infantry fire from some over anxious Federal troops just behind the *12th*.

The situation may sound worse than it actually was. The *12th Ohio* did not suffer severely during the encounter, losing 30 men out of 200 engaged and most of these from artillery fire. Whether the *12th*'s inability to press forward was justifiable or not, the failure led to severe repercussions for the other regiments of Ewing's brigade. Because the *12th Ohio* could not advance and clear out the Confederates from the 40-Acre Cornfield, Gregg's South Carolinians were left in an enviable position to enfilade the rest of Ewing's brigade. Between Gregg's flanking fire and Confederate counterattack in their front, the *30th* and *23rd Ohio* found themselves in a desperate situation.

The two other regiments on the *12th Ohio*'s left caught the brunt of an attack by elements of the Confederate counterattack. The *30th Ohio* took the harshest beating. Its course took it through the northern portion of the 40-Acre Cornfield, passing over carnage from the *16th Connecticut*'s fight, to reach the stone wall along the cornfield's northwestern front. There the Ohioans primarily faced Archer's attack emerging from the Harper's Ferry Road 300 yards away, while at the same time Gregg's South Carolinians sniped away at their exposed left flank. During the desperate encounter, the regiment lost 80 men including the unit's commander Lieutenant Colonel Theodore Jones, captured at the cornfield's stone wall, and five other officers. While both the bearers of the national and regimental colors were shot down, the flags were retrieved and carried safely to the rear.

Archer's men rushed forward upon the stone wall while the *30th* and *23rd Ohio* made them pay freely in blood for each step, cutting down a third of the force including the 14th Tennessee's Colonel William McComb. After gaining the wall, Archer's Brigade pressed roughly 100 yards into the 40-Acre Cornfield only to get battered back by some of the *30th*'s survivors rallying with some stubborn members of the *16th Connecticut*. Archer's bloodied ranks retreated to take cover behind the wall while members of the 12th South Carolina flushed out the remaining Ohioans from the 40-Acre Cornfield, a costly act since their commander, Colonel Barnes, was mortally wounded in the effort.

The *23rd Ohio* fared little better than its fellow units after it engaged the enemy on the western side of the plowed field beyond the Otto Farm Lane and north of the 40-Acre Cornfield. While directing the *23rd*, the regiment's commander, Major J. M. Comley, was also deceived by the Confederate attackers in Yankee blue, thinking them to be Union troops and having his troops withhold their fire while the enemy advanced. Eventually, the regiment was forced to fall back from its position along the plowed field before the oncoming ranks of Jones's men led by Toombs.

With the *IX Corps'* left flank rolled up, Major General Cox ordered his troops to fall back from their position outside of Sharpsburg, thus surrendering the ground they had spent freely in blood and effort to take. Fairchild's brigade and Willcox's division were to retreat while Sturgis's men were to be reemployed to fill the gap caused by Rodman's collapsing line. In the meantime, the Confederates in Jones's and Hill's command jubilantly forged on in their counterattack. Meanwhile, other Confederate forces came back in the fray. Upon learning of the Federal repulse, Garnett gathered what forces he could find and advanced to the front. The setback was so complete for the *IX Corps*, it was hard to believe its advance from the bridge had been seemingly so inexorable nor that the forces that opposed it had been so few.

Each of the *IX Corps'* brigades that had successfully assailed the Confederate line fell back in the face of the Confederate onslaught. For the *9th New York Zouaves* the call to retire was especially bitter given their exhausting bloody charge just a short while before. Now they were being asked to give up the ground that they and their comrades had sacrificed so much to gain. No one probably responded with greater indignation at the suggestion of retreating than the regiment's commander, Lieutenant Colonel Kimball. When a staff officer from Willcox's division, Major L. C. Brackett, arrived to inform Kimball of the need to withdraw due to the deteriorating situation on the corps' left and rear, the colonel strongly objected. He adamantly believed troops were still on his left and together with these and his own command Sharpsburg could be taken and Lee's right rank crushed or, in the alternative, his regiment could at least hold his current position. Kimball chastised Brackett to report to the generals that an advance should be ordered not a retreat. Brackett didn't feel he had the authority to overrule Colonel Kimball, but some of the *9th New York's* officers tried to convince their commander that the staff officer's report of the situation was correct and, especially since the regiment was low on ammunition, a retreat should be called. "We have bayonets," the Colonel roared defiantly, "What are they given to us for?" Finally, General Willcox himself rode up to the scene and overruled Kimball's zeal. Just as the retreat was about to get under way, a large contingent of enemy troops was spied preparing for a charge on the Zouaves. Willcox feared the *9th New York* might be overwhelmed as there were no reinforcements the regiment could call upon for aid nor was there any extra ammunition nearby to replace the soldiers' exhausted supply. Willcox inquired of Kimball, "Ask your command if they will receive the charge at the point of the bayonet if we stick to them." When so queried, the New Yorkers voiced the affirmative with cheers and fixed their bayonets. Fortunately, the regiment's elan was not so desperately tested as the Confederate threat vaporized due to needs elsewhere on the field. With the danger from the enemy passed, the Zouaves fell back to safer ground. As the *9th New York* withdrew, Kimball refused to acknowledge that his command had been defeated. He called out to General Willcox, "Look at my regiment! They go off this field under orders. They are not driven off. Do they look like a beaten regiment?"

If the *9th New York* did not look beaten, events on the battlefield showed the *IX Corps* was being bested by its numerically inferior adversaries. Remarkably, the Confederates had snatched victory from the proverbial jaws of defeat and Burnside's force was on the retreat on the entire front. Now Jones's and Hill's forces moved forward to drive the fleeing *IX Corps* into the Antietam Creek.

CHAPTER 14

STAND OF THE *IX CORPS*

THE COMMISSION OF EWING'S *Kanawha Division 1st Brigade* was not the final effort to contest the Confederate tide. Units from Sturgis's division engaged earlier in the day rejoined the fighting, advancing from its covered positions behind the ridge to take up the space created by Harland's brigade's disintegration and the repulse of Ewing's brigade. Some of these troops were still low on ammunition and would have to rely on the bayonet when they expended their last cartridge.

Nagle's brigade was on the left flank moving forward with the *48th Pennsylvania* and *9th New Hampshire*, leaving the two regiments cut up in the bridge assault, the *2nd Maryland* and the *6th New Hampshire*, behind as a reserve. The *9th New Hampshire* was detailed to go into the 40-Acre Cornfield where the *12th Ohio* was still engaged. The New Hampshire men entered the corn rows only to meet the same fate that its predecessors had suffered there and fell back to the creek. With the retreat of the *9th New Hampshire*, the Federals finally quit the 40-Acre Cornfield.

On Nagle's right, most of Ferrero's brigade advanced toward the Otto Farm Lane overlooking the plowed field and ravine north of the 40-Acre Cornfield. General Cox threw the *35th Massachusetts* into the fray himself. Originally, Colonel Ferrero had detailed the unit to block stragglers fleeing from frontline units. Desperate to thwart the Confederate advance, Cox employed the command more aggressively, overruling Ferrero's orders and having the unit move forward. The Massachusetts troops pressed

The Otto Farm ravine where the *35th Massachusetts* engaged in a firefight with the advancing Rebels.

ahead all the way to the Otto Farm Lane where they took cover behind the fence along the road and blasted a volley at Confederate units under Toombs. Confederate troops lined up behind the fences on the western edge of plowed field, 300 yards off to the west and returned fire. It was the beginning of a long firefight that would continue throughout the waning daylight hours.

The rest of Ferrero's brigade went into position south of the *35th Massachusetts*, but did not choose to get severely involved and did not advance all the way to the Otto Farm Lane. The regiment did offer some fire, enough to completely deplete the *51st Pennsylvania*'s ammunition supply. This event resulted in orders for the *51st* to be pulled out of the line and replaced by the *48th Pennsylvania* from Nagle's brigade.

Union artillery was also in action trying to curb the Rebel

momentum. One battery so involved was Muhlenberg's *Battery A* of the *5th U.S. Artillery* on the far left of the *IX Corps* line. This was ordered across the Lower Bridge by Brigadier General Cox himself with directions to report to Brigadier General Rodman during the attack against Jones's line. That general had sent Muhlenberg to his threatened left to counter the enemy's flank attack, the battery going into position south of Durrell's and Cook's batteries and east of the 40-Acre Cornfield. The lieutenant set up his guns within 600 yards of some Confederate troops and opened up on them with spherical case and shell. As the enemy troops came on, Muhlenberg began to fret to his cannoneers about the lack of infantry to support. With the opposing infantry closing within 100 yards of the battery's Napoleons, the artillery officer pulled his command back only to find the enemy moving in from the left while Confederate shells began to explode around him. The pressure proved too great to be withstood without some help and Muhlenberg retreated his guns to safety over the Lower Bridge to the opposite bank of the Antietam.

Coffin's section also participated in withstanding the Confederate counterattack. After assisting Willcox's advance from the Otto Farm Orchard, he moved farther south where he came under fire from Richardson's Confederate battery. Finally, advancing Confederate infantry and low ammunition forced the feisty Coffin to retreat. Also forced to retreat were Durrell's and Clark's batteries, both low on ammunition.

The oncoming evening and D. R. Jones's reluctance to press the offensive much further allowed the fighting to gradually subside. Jones's decision was not popular. Other commanders were confident, both on the field and long afterwards, that they could have pushed the *IX Corps* into the Antietam Creek. Such ardor was, perhaps, overly ambitious. True, the *IX Corps* was forced back, but it still held a substantial advantage in manpower. Jones was not so much overly cautious as he realized the limits of the troops he had on hand. They had already performed a significant feat in forcing the enemy to fall back. It would be futile to unleash them to try to reach for the unobtainable.

Just as the *IX Corps* had been forced to cower on the heights over the Lower Bridge, so too was the Federal artillery on the field suffering humiliation at the hands of their counterparts. By now the Confederates had managed to amass as many as 43 guns on the scene and McIntosh's guns had been reclaimed and were returned to service. From their advantageous firing positions on the high ground south of Sharpsburg, they combined to unleash a cannonade overpowering the Federal gunners, even forcing some to meekly withdraw for cover. This misfortune was compounded by another difficulty. Union long-range guns had run low on ammunition trying to suppress the fire of the enemy throughout the day so that they were limited in the shots they could return to the other side of the Antietam. Muhlenberg's guns were even forced to the absurd expedient of popping away with blanks.

The maneuvering and shifting of lines and ranks to gain advantage and victory was coming to an end. The situation for the *IX Corps* was no longer desperate, but neither was it particularly auspicious. About an hour and a half after the corps had begun its grand advance to crush the enemy right, at 1630 its offensive had reached its apex and was beginning to be turned back. By 1700, Burnside's command was hugging the high ground west of the Lower Bridge, its gains lost and opportunities squandered. For this the *IX Corps* lost around 2,350 men during the day's fighting. The Confederate cost for thwarting the Federals at what should have been their finest hour was relatively inexpensive. A. P. Hill's command lost only 63 killed and 346 wounded in the attack of his brigades. Even despite the setback, Burnside still had the advantage in number of men he could field, still outnumbering Hill's and Jones's ranks combined and certainly having enough men to challenge the Confederates' recent gains. Moreover the *IX Corps* was not alone. Other troops were nearby that could have provided support, the most significant of which was Porter's *V Corps* located to the northeast at the Middle Bridge. But even with all this power on hand, no effort was made to sweep back the victorious Confederate tide.

Even though the *IX Corps* had suffered a frustrating setback, its commanders sought to knit the battlefield's events into a tapestry of victory. Burnside put the most positive spin on his repulse in his after-action report, "It being apparent that the enemy was strongly re-enforced, and that we could not be re-enforced, the command was ordered to fall back to the crests above the bridge, which movement was performed in the most perfect order under cover of batteries on the height, the same formation being adopted that was made before the attack."

McClellan summed up the *IX Corps'* setback by also noting the supposed infusion of new Confederate troops, "The fresh troops of the enemy pouring in, and the accumulation of artillery against this command, destroyed all hopes of accomplishing anything more." Of the final situation southeast of Sharpsburg, the most accurate assessment was made by a very relieved D. R. Jones. He triumphantly recorded of the battle's outcome, "Night had now come on, putting an end to the conflict, and leaving my command in the possession of the ground we had held in the morning, with the exception of the mere bridge."

BATTLEFIELD INFORMATION AND TOUR

The Antietam National Battlefield Park

The Antietam National Cemetery predates the battlefield by almost 30 years, it being created shortly before the war had concluded when the state of Maryland purchased land to inter the bodies of those who died during the battle. In August 1890, Antietam became the second battlefield to be preserved by the United States War Department following the first, Chickamauga and Chattanooga, by little more than a week. Unlike the Chickamauga and Gettysburg battlefields, the Federal government did not choose to buy up large tracts of land to form the park. Instead, small plots were acquired for memorial tablets along the roads and avenues that traced some of the fight's troop positions. This method was attractive to Federal authorities since it was quicker and cheaper than the wholesale purchase of land. In 1933, the War Department turned maintenance of battlefields over to the Department of the Interior and the National Park Service. Afterward, the government's strategy toward preserving the field changed and it began to accept donations of land and make purchases of significant tracts.

The battle actually encompassed nearly 1,800 acres of land outside Sharpsburg much of which the National Park Service now owns. There are more than eight miles of road allowing tourists to drive an auto route with designated stops at the most important points of the fighting. Various markers can be found on the field to help the visitor understand the action that took place during the battle of Antietam. National Park Service "Waysides," colorful informational signs, have been placed at the numbered auto tour stops, and include maps, pictures, quotes from significant figures, and a general overview of important moments during the battle. Also scattered about the field are some 300 cast-iron tablets placed on the field by the War Department describing the positions and detailing the movements and actions of regiments, brigades, and divisions. The information is more detailed than that found on the Waysides and sometimes require a more in-depth knowledge of the battle. More than one hundred monuments have been placed on the field inviting remembrance of the feats by various units that struggled throughout the day. The vast majority of these are dedicated to Union regiments. Only a handful note the service of Confederate troops. Finally, inverted cannon barrels standing in stone blocks mark the places where general officers on both sides were either killed or mortally wounded. A total of six generals were so injured on 17 September 1862—two in the Burnside's Bridge sector: Confederate Brigadier General L. O'Brien Branch and Federal Brigadier General Isaac P. Rodman.

A variety of public and private groups have endeavored to protect the field from the encroachment of development. In particular, The Conservation Fund recently assisted in the acquisition of the Roulette Farm near Bloody Lane. To learn more about The Conservation Fund's battlefield preservation program, write: The Civil War Battlefield Campaign, 1800 North Kent Street, Suite 1120, Arlington, VA 22209. There are also ways to help with the preservation of some of Antietam's landmarks. The Adopt-a-Monument program encourages individuals, organizations and companies to "adopt" monuments on the Antietam National Battlefield and assist efforts to protect and preserve the park's 92 monuments. For more information call (301) 432-7672 or write: Adopt-a-Monument, Antietam National Battlefield, P.O. Box 158, Sharpsburg, MD 21782. Another preservation effort involves the many artillery pieces from the battlefield, placed there during the 1950s and 1960s by the Adopt-A-Cannon Program. Repairing damage to carriages from the elements and other factors is an expensive task. For more information call 301-432-7672 or write: Antietam National Battlefield, Adopt-A-Cannon Program, P. O. Box 158, Sharpsburg, Maryland 21782.

The Visitor's Center

The Antietam National Battlefield Park's Visitor Center should be the first stop on a battlefield tour. The center contains a museum displaying artifacts from the battle such as a breast plate worn by an officer as protection against bullets, uniforms, and weapons; an observation room providing a view of the ground over which much of the battle was fought, except of course Burnside's Bridge; a research center with first-hand material; and a bookstore selling Antietam and Civil War related books and maps, postcards, and other memorabilia. The center also boasts a 134-seat theater that shows a movie entitled "Antietam Visit" which details the battle and President Abraham Lincoln's visit with Major General George Brinton McClellan on 1 October 1862. The Visitor Center is open every day except Thanksgiving, Christmas, and New Year's Day. Its hours are June–August, 8:30 a.m. to 6:00 p.m.; and September–May, 8:30 a.m. to 5:00 p.m. To contact the park write or call: Antietam National Battlefield, P.O. Box 158 Sharpsburg, MD 21782-0158; phone numbers: Programs and Information–(301)-432-5124; Superintendent and Administration–(301)-432-7672; Internet: www.nps.gov/anti/

Events at the Antietam National Battlefield and Sharpsburg

The Park Service holds events throughout the year including talks, tours, and living history demonstrations. A variety of events are scheduled around the anniversary of the battle on 17 September. An excellent and informative way of getting to know the battlefield are ranger-led tours of significant areas on the battlefield that take place at approximately the same time the events occurred there during the fighting. These talks provide moving accounts of the Civil War experience and the horror that combat of that era held for its participants. Usually taking place around the battle's anniversary is the Sharpsburg Heritage Festival. This features tours of Sharpsburg, Civil War living history events with Union and Confederate soldiers, concerts, crafts, plenty of food, and even a barn dance. An important day on the Antietam calendar not revolving around the actual day of the battle takes place in December when the Annual Memorial Illumination is held. This is a moving event during which some 23,000 candles are placed on the battlefield grounds and lit, each one representing a casualty from both sides that fought during the battle.

Tour of the Burnside's Bridge Sector

Understanding any battlefield is best achieved by foot. Walking provides opportunities to observe the terrain as soldiers actually experienced it during the battle and allows time to reflect on the engagements of various units, read markers and scan monuments. If you choose to hike the roads, be sure to keep on the shoulder and out of the way of other traffic. However, the Antietam battlefield is quite large and even covering the terrain over which the Burnside's Bridge action was fought in this manner can take hours. Riding through the park by bicycle may be a better option. Cyclists should wear a helmet and take care when descending the steep hills on the route. Traveling the field by automobile allows the speediest, and easiest, transport from site to site. When stopping your car on the road, make sure your vehicle is well on the shoulder along side it. The undulating ground that made the battle confusing for Union and Confederate troops can also make it difficult

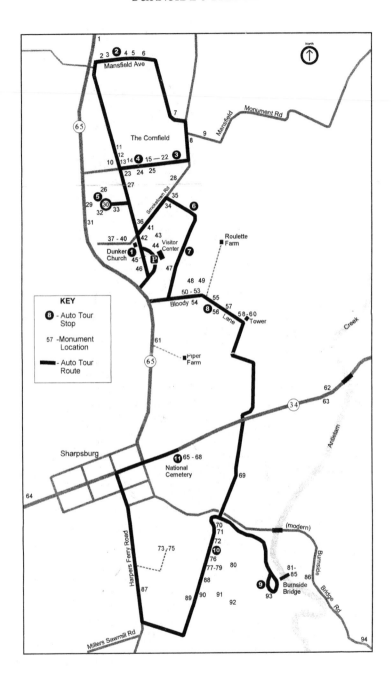

for drivers to see obstructions in the road until they are almost upon them.

The sector covered in *Burnside's Bridge* can be reached from the Visitor's Center by either taking a right from the parking lot, another right on the Smoketown Road, and then the next right. This route will take you past most of the action associated with Bloody Lane. Once you pass the intersection with the Boonsboro Pike, you will be in the Burnside's Bridge sector. This can also be reached by taking a left from the Visitor's Center parking lot, a left on Route 65 back into Sharpsburg, then a left on Route 34, the Boonsboro Pike, and finally a right on the park road that takes you into the sector. This one-way park road, Rodman Avenue, follows the path of the old Sherrick Farm Lane.

The section of the battlefield you are entering is perhaps best viewed from the National Cemetery on the heights to your right, but you will want to get acquainted with the markers and monuments here first to make them out from that location. Not far from the beginning of Rodman Avenue, on the left of the road, is a marker that describes the involvement of Poland's *U.S. Regulars* in the fight, its position extended south from the Boonsboro Turnpike. It held this position here for some time before eventually falling back and crossing the Middle Bridge to the east. To your right is a tablet noting Garnett's position nearly halfway between the cemetery wall and the road. There his troops waited for Christ's attack in the Sherrick cornfield that extended in a wide belt before the National Cemetery almost to the Lower Bridge Road off to the south.

About halfway down the road, roughly a third of a mile, is a monument with an officer looking west holding binoculars. This belongs to the *50th Pennsylvania* and cites the counties from which the regiment's troops were recruited, its casualties suffered during the battle and later engagements. Pennsylvania's monuments on this part of the field are either delightfully allegorical or represent a prominent figure in the battlefield. The person depicted here is none other than Colonel Benjamin C. Christ, commander of the

1st *Brigade* of Willcox's division and the former leader of the *50th Pennsylvania* before the battle of Antietam. A tablet beside the statue notes that Christ's brigade was checked near here. Christ's men made an awkward stand until Welsh's *2nd Brigade*, also with Willcox's *2nd Division*, had moved up far enough to allow their comrades to continue. Elements of Christ's command then drove up onto the heights where the cemetery is now and halted before being ordered by Cox to withdraw due to the deteriorating situation on the *IX Corps'* left.

Continuing down the road, you will find several markers just before a bridge crossing the Burnside's Bridge Road leading to Sharpsburg. The ones to the left overlook the Sherrick House and tell of Welsh's advance and the involvement of Lieutenant John N. Coffin's section of the *8th Massachusetts Artillery*. At this point, Welsh's brigade, beginning its march near the Antietam Creek on the left of Burnside's Bridge Road by this point had come astride the road leading to Sharpsburg with its left west and its right east of the road. A sign gives the general direction to Burnside's Bridge, a thousand yards distant, which can also be roughly located by tracing the Burnside's Bridge Road leading south just ahead of you. To the right of the road are markers describing the action involving Jenkins' Brigade at the stone house which can be seen a short distance up the Burnside's Bridge Road toward the town, and the orchard located near there. It was in this vicinity that the *17th Michigan* from Christ's brigade and the right of Welsh's brigade fought off members of Jenkins' Brigade and Colonel F. W. McMaster's 17th South Carolina and the Holcombe Legion in an apple orchard to the right of the house and mill with help from Coffin's guns which were 350 yards to the south close to the Otto House. Jenkins's Brigade under Walker was forced to fall back to the edge of Sharpsburg while McMaster's troops held out in the stone house and stone mill for a while longer until they too were compelled to retreat.

Continue over the bridge, take a left to head toward

Burnside's Bridge. The road descends through the Lower Bridge Road Ravine as you approach the Antietam Creek and then ascends to a parking lot located on the bluffs above the stream. This is the formidable position occupied by the 2nd and 20th Georgia overlooking Burnside's Bridge. There are two designated places from which to view the ground held by the Georgians. One directly ahead can be reached from steps leading from the parking lot. From here the bridge can be seen from above the remnants of entrenchments dug by the Georgians to strengthen their position. A Wayside sign entitled "Point Blank Range" tells the story of the Confederate defense here and displays a picture of the indomitable Robert Augustus Toombs who commanded the defenses of the Antietam crossing here. Another viewpoint from the Georgian position can be reached by a path leading off to the right marked by signs pointing to "Georgian Overlook." This leads to a plaque that provides a brief overview of Burnside's doomed attack. The point itself overlooks the locations from which the *11th Connecticut* and Nagle's brigade launched their ill-fated attacks. A dirt path continues to the right leading to the Snavely's Ford Trail that will be discussed later.

A cement path and steps lead down to Burnside's Bridge itself and the sandy trail traces the path that the Lower Bridge Road took over this ground. Once over the bridge on to the eastern side of the Antietam, the visitor is met with a series of stubby monuments belonging to the *21st Massachusetts, 35th Massachusetts,* and *51st Pennsylvania* of Fererro's *2nd Division, 2nd Brigade* and the *2nd Maryland* of Nagle's *2nd Division, 1st Brigade.* The most imposing monument here is that of the *51st New York* that contains a plaque containing the state seal and a description of the bridge action. Tablets on either side of the New York monument also tell of the bridge assaults, specifically discussing the part of Ferrero's brigade.

Continue down the sandy path along the Antietam Creek. It is easy to see as you go how Union troops making their assaults against the bridge from this direction were such easy targets to the Georgians entrenched on the bluffs on the opposite side of the stream. At the third break in the wooden fence that follows the road, a plaque notes that Nagle's *1st Brigade* made their charge into the road here, heading north toward the bridge. Advance through the gap heading straight ahead toward the trees and up the base of the ridge there. Behind some trees is hidden the monument to the *11th Connecticut*, bearing a bas relief depiction of their fateful move on the bridge. The daring Captain Griswold can be seen on the left wading through the Antietam, sword in hand, urging on his comrades. On the back is a roster of those in the regiment killed during the battle listed by company. A marker gives the details of the *11th Connecticut*'s action, telling that their path took them over the eastern part of the spur and reached the banks of the stream. The regiment's Colonel Kingsbury fell not far from where you are standing.

After recrossing the bridge to the western side of the Antietam, a dirt path can be seen leading south along the stream's path. This is the two-and-one-half-mile Snavely Ford trail, a pleasant walk along the winding Antietam Creek. A brochure can be obtained from a wooden post at the beginning of the trail. This contains historical information on the battle as well as points of natural interest as well. Sites are marked along the trail with numbered posts corresponding to sections of the brochure. Of great interest is the depth of the Antietam and the terrain on both sides of the stream since both played a great roll in blocking the Federal crossing to the western side. A sign marks the location of Snavely's Ford, the point at which Rodman's division crossed the stream, and the path begins to wind up the Otto Farm ravine northward eventually reaching the parking lot. A quicker way to Snavely's Ford for those who do not wish to take the entire walk is to take the trail in reverse, starting from the parking lot heading south until you reach the ford.

Once back at the parking lot, note the monument just to the south. This is the McKinley Monument, an obelisk with a woman holding a wreath above a bas relief of William McKinley as he appeared when he was a youth during the Civil War and his more elderly countenance as president of the United States. Another bas relief shows a stately McKinley placidly standing and passing out a cup of coffee to troops crouching for cover. The monument also carries an inscription noting the service for which the future president was commended on the Antietam battlefield:

> Sergeant McKinley, Company E, 23rd Ohio Volunteer Infantry while in charge of the Commissary Department, on the afternoon of the day of the battle of Antietam, September, 17, 1862, personally and without orders served hot coffee and warm food to every man in the regiment on this spot; and in doing so had to pass under fire.

The monument also notes the dates of McKinley's many political posts.

Behind the parking lot is where the Federal line would have been after it finally crossed the bridge extending from the south over to the north beyond the road leading to Burnside's Bridge. Beyond, over the undulating ground to the crest out in the west, is the ground that Rodman's division had to pass during its attack. The houses and the water tower in the distance help mark out the path of the Harper's Ferry Road as it leads into Sharpsburg.

Leave the parking lot, returning north toward Sharpsburg. On the way, just as the road turns toward Sharpsburg is a marker detailing the part Willcox's *1st Division* played in the action. The marker notes that both of Willcox's brigades were deployed in this vicinity before they made their march toward Sharpsburg. Christ's *1st Brigade* was situated on the low ground between the bluff and the creek while Welsh's *2nd Brigade* was positioned on the bluffs to the left.

When you return to the vicinity of the overpass over the Burnside's Bridge Road, which will be on your right, you will pass a series of monuments to the left. Turn left on Branch Avenue which is a one-way route. Branch Avenue is a cornucopia of monuments and tablets following the northern extent where the plowed field and the 40-Acre Cornfield once lay on the Otto Farm. To the left the ground pitches downward into the Otto Ravine and to the left the land rolls upward to the high ground before Harper's Ferry Road where the D. R. Jones line consisted of Drayton's and Kemper's Brigades. Most visitors tend to speed through this section of the field in their automobiles, pausing momentarily to scan the tablets or read a monument. This is unfortunate since along this route is where some of the battle's most dramatic action took place. The visitor may want to stop at various points along the avenue and take some moments to inspect the landmarks and landscape here.

The most suitable stop is at auto tour site point 10 where several monuments and tablets are also located. Take a moment to walk over and view the monuments that you passed earlier. The one with a granite soldier on top biting a cartridge with such grit belongs to the *45th Pennsylvania*. The purpose of this statue was to remind future generations used to modern breechloading weapons the manner that most Civil War soldiers loaded their ammunition.

The next monument of a stalwart bareheaded soldier holding a musket is the subject of some creative visualization. This is supposed to represent a battlefield survivor who had been placed on evening picket duty in a post of some danger. The monument belongs to the *100th Pennsylvania* and is emblazoned with their sobriquet, "The Roundheads." Another monument remembers the *36th Ohio* that lost its colonel, Melvin Clarke near here. This ground was on the path of Welsh's *2nd Brigade* as it moved up against Sharpsburg along with Christ's *1st Brigade*, the command beginning to veer over the Lower Bridge Road as it progressed. The "Roundheads" of the *100th Pennsylvania* were in advance of the main line, acting as skirmishers. Crook's *1st Brigade* of the Kanawha was in the rear providing support.

Returning to the parking area, two Wayside signs detail

some of the action at Antietam and its outcome. The one entitled "Forever Free" provides some brief information about the aftermath of the battle, in particular the part the Union "victory" played in the Emancipation Proclamation's issuance. "It is A. P. Hill" tells of the retreat of D. R. Jones' stroops, with a quotation from Private Dooley, and the Light Division's counterattack. Markers here designate the actions of Willcox's and Rodman's division as well as the advance of Crook's *Kanawha Division, 2nd Brigade*. On the other side of the road are markers detailing the positions and activities of D. R. Jones's brigades, in particular Drayton's Brigade which would have been on the crest of the hill beyond. A sign also points out the direction of Kemper's Brigade which was on the right of Drayton.

Looking off in the distance across the Otto Farm Ravine in front of you, you will be able to see a white block on the other edge of the depression, the monument to the *11th Ohio*. Near the monument you will also see a slight trace of the Otto Farm Lane on the ground. The lane zigzagged near the point where the *11th Ohio*'s monument now stands and headed south along the ravine. You can trace its approximate course with the help of the other monuments located in the fields east of Branch Avenue.

Continuing down Branch Avenue are tablets designating the actions of *Kanawha Division* regiments that struggled to fend off Hill's Confederates after they had broken the Federal left held by Harland's brigade. The first tablet shows the position of the *23rd Ohio* of Ewing's brigade which reached the point where the modern stone wall borders the road, then the northern border of the large plowed field on the Otto Farm, its right near the tablet's current position and the left of the regiment extending hundreds of yards to the southwest. From his position here, Major J. M. Comley commanding the regiment saw the Confederates dressed in Federal blue operating on his left that soon put his men under a fierce flanking fire.

After this, on the other side of the road is a tablet telling the story of Kemper's Brigade which had advanced to the high ground before the Harper's Ferry Road to meet the Federal attack. A sign here also points out the direction of Drayton's Brigade. These should be read in conjunction with the tablet on the left-hand side of the road telling the story of Fairchild's advance. Note its oblique arc beginning its charge 450 yards east of the tablet beyond the ravine and then veering 400 yards northwest toward Sharpsburg as his regiments came on striking and breaking Kemper's and Drayton's Brigades when it climbed up the steep ascent where the Confederates were situated.

The next tablet on the left tells the story of the *35th Massachusetts'* desperate stand on the other side of the ravine to the east. There it took position in the wake of the *IX Corps* retreat and in the face of the many Confederate brigades falling upon them. The regiment maintained its position under severe enemy fire in the vicinity of Branch Avenue until finally forced to retreat.

The *35th*'s tablet is followed by the *51st Pennsylvania*'s second monument on the field, a skirmisher holding a rifle with a clenched fist. Next is the monument to *Durrell's Independent Battery D* of the *Pennsylvania Light Artillery*, showing a gunner with rolled-up sleeves holding a ramrod in one hand and the other hand held over his eyes like a visor. The battery of six 10-pound parrott rifles had been located just east of the Otto Farm Lane.

Just beyond is another monument placed on the field by men from the *48th Pennsylvania*. The bronze figure you see is Brigadier General James Nagle who originally commanded the regiment as its colonel. Nagle's son modeled for the sculptor's work wearing his father's uniform. A tablet discusses the *48th*'s replacement of the battered *51st Pennsylvania* in the Federal line of battle after the bridge had been taken.

To the right are found markers of the Confederate action including a tablet telling of Branch's Brigade and the death of Branch. An inverted cannon farther ahead purportedly marks the place where Branch was killed while talking to fellow Brigadier General James Archer. Branch had been bringing his North Carolina brigade into the fray when he was hit.

The next several markers on the left belong to more *Kanawha* regiments and their place in the action. The first tells of Ewing's brigade and that it retreated east of the tablets after attempting to stay the Confederate counterattack. Farther along is the monument to the *30th Ohio* which was made in the guise of a castle tower wrapped in a flag and a wreath laid under its battlements. The *30th* made it as far as a stone wall here before, like the rest of the brigade, it was forced to retreat due to heavy flanking fire from the left.

The next tablet tells of Rodman's engagement, in particular the unfortunate fate of Harland's brigade. The brigade split apart in the vicinity of the tablet with the *8th Connecticut* veering off to the northwest, just south of the obelisk, and the *4th Rhode Island* and the *16th Connecticut* remaining in the 40-Acre Cornfield, marked by a sign not far ahead, where they were hit in flank by Gregg's Brigade. Beyond this another tablet gives a more specific description of the *8th Connecticut's* passing onward up the heights outside of Sharpsburg while the remaining regiments stayed in the 40-Acre Cornfield.

Unfortunately, the geography of the 40-Acre Cornfield is almost as impenetrable to view from Branch Avenue as it was to Union troops during the battle. Corn no longer is grown here, but scrubby trees block the ground's descent into the Otto Farm Ravine. A better glimpse of the terrain can sometimes be had from the high ground along the Harper's Ferry Road.

The next few tablets on the left of the road, before it bends sharply to the west toward the Harper's Ferry Road, give the dispositions of Federal artillery during the battle. Captain J. C. Clark's *4th U.S. Artillery, Battery E* was south of Durrell's Pennsylvania battery and east of the 40-Acre Cornfield with four more 10-pound parrott rifles that were used to pound D. R. Jones's position. First Lieutenant Samuel N. Benjamin's *2nd U.S Artillery, Battery E* was located on the heights on the eastern side of the Antietam Creek. The next tablet marks the placement of Lieutenant Marcus P. Miller's *Battery G* of the *4th U.S. Artillery* which was not actively engaged in the fighting. This was not the case with *Battery A* of the *5th U.S. Artillery* under Lieutenant Charles P. Muhlenburg the subject of the third tablet. At first employed to blast the Georgian position over the Lower Bridge, the battery operated east of this point attempting to stem the Confederate flank attack until forced to withdraw due to the combined threat of advancing Confederate infantry and a bombardment from enemy guns.

The tablet on the right side of the road is quite significant and lends one to pause. This tells the story of Gregg's Brigade, how it formed to the southwest and then swung into the south and western faces of the 40-Acre Cornfield 100 yards east of this point. From there it moved on to over-whelm the hapless *16th Connecticut* and tap the entire left flank of the *IX Corps* attacking line. Another position to consider the ground of Gregg's advance is at the end of Branch Avenue where it intersects with the Harper's Ferry Road as will be seen below.

Another tablet to the left of the road at the angle where the road heads west toward the Harper's Ferry Road tells the position of John Walker's division to the southeast of this point. Walker's Division was sent north to reinforce Jackson's forces playing an instrumental role in the unin-tentional ambush of Sedgwick's *2nd Division* of the *II Corps* in the West Wood. It is a telling indication of how Lee weakened his left to bolster his right that he left such a long stretch of ground vacant before the *IX Corps* which was over 12,000 men strong.

Continue up the remainder of Branch Avenue, stopping at the guns and next group of tablets where the road ends at the Harper's Ferry Road. From here you can better visu-alize Gregg's part in A. P. Hill's counterattack. This would have passed on the ground before you moving roughly from the south to the north through the 40-Acre Cornfield. These troops had come up the Miller Sawmill Road, which intersects with the Harper's Ferry Road a short distance to the south behind you, veered south to avoid Federal artillery, and then formed in fields east of the Harper's Ferry Road. Then the brigade marched into the 40-Acre Cornfield from the southwest, its northernmost extent being defined by Branch Avenue. The regiments of Branch's Brigade on Gregg's left made a more haphazard appearance on the battlefield. Generally though, Branch's command paralleled Branch Avenue as it heads into the Harper's Ferry Road, before curving to the east, again paralleling Branch Avenue but this time as it runs along the Otto Farm Ravine.

Tablets here also mark the positions of A. P. Hill's artillery. The most prominent group of guns noted here are those of McIntosh's batteries which set up 400 yards to the north and 100 yards to the east, on the edge of the plateau off to your left. These were the guns that arrived from A. P. Hill's Light Division in time to play a part in the climax of the *IX Corps* attack. McIntosh's gunners managed to pepper away at the oncoming Federal lines, but were forced to flee from their pieces by the oncoming *8th Connecticut*. The guns were later recaptured and turned once again on the Federals as they retreated. The other artillery positions mentioned here are A. P. Hill, Purcell (Virginia) Artillery (Pegram's battery) stationed here on the high ground and Crenshaw's (Virginia) battery stationed farther to the south, both commanding a wide view allowing them to harass the enemy. Braxton's battery or the Fredericksburg (Virginia) Artillery was stationed in the vicinity of Gregg's left, 270 yards south and 130 yards east of your position.

Turn right on the Harper's Ferry Road. Continue onward until you come to the next series of tablets. These show the Harper's Ferry Road line once A.P. Hill's Light Division had reached the field. Archer's Brigade went forward to collide into the high-watermark of the Federal advance with the forces Toombs had scrounged up on his left.

Continue up the road until you see a brown park sign for the *Hawkin's Zouave* monument. Pull off the road onto the shoulder as best you can. This is one of the more awkward sites on the battlefield situated as it is on a sliver of land in-between private property. Follow the path as it heads east and then north to the imposing obelisk dedicated to the *9th New York*. The Federals came from the southeast, heading northwest, eventually breaking the Confederate line here. To the northwest, Sharpsburg can be seen and a plaque shows a drawing with the victorious New Yorkers taking the stone wall from which their enemy had sought cover, the Confederates fleeing toward the town.

Southeast of the Zouave monument and on private ground is a plain monument to the *8th Connecticut* which made its own lone stand in the face of a fierce Confederate counterattack. Also situated there is another somber memorial to a fallen officer, the inverted cannon barrel. This one is dedicated to Isaac Rodman who was mortally wounded 265 yards south of the marker.

If you continue on the Harper's Ferry Road this will take you back into the town of Sharpsburg. From there you may want to head east on the Boonsboro Turnpike to the National Cemetery. Heading directly straight through the cemetery once you pass its gates and the formidable statue in your front. Beyond a slight ramp can be found that provides a viewpoint over the wall there. From this position can be seen the ground over which the fighting north of the Lower Bridge Road took place. Just before you can be seen Rodman Avenue or the former Sherrick Farm Lane.

BIBLIOGRAPHY

Alexander, E. Porter. *Memoirs of a Confederate.* New York: Scribner's, 1907.

Bilby, Joseph G. *Civil War Firearms: Their Historical Background, Tactical Use and Modern Collecting and Shooting.* Conshohocken, PA: Combined Publishing, 1996.

Blakeslee, Bernard F. *History of the 16th Connecticut Volunteers.* Hartford: The Case, 1875.

Bosbyshell, Oliver C. *The 48th in the War.* Philadelphia, 1895.

Child, William. *A History of the Fifth Regiment New Hampshire Volunteers, in the American Civil War, 1861–65.* Bristol, NH: Musgrove, 1893.

Cox, Jacob D. *Military Reminiscences of the Civil War.* 2 volumes. New York: Scribner's, 1900.

Crater, Lewis. *History of the Fiftieth Regiment, Pennsylvania Veteran Volunteers, 1861-65.* Reading: Coleman Printing House, 1884.

Cannan, John. *The Antietam Campaign: August–September 1862,* Revised and Expanded Edition. Conshohocken, PA: Combined Publishing, 1990, 1994.

Carman, Ezra A. Battle of Antietam Manuscript. Manuscript Division. Library of Congress, Washington, DC.

Carman, Ezra A. Letters. Carman Collection. Manuscript and Rare Book Section. New York Public Library, New York, NY.

Dooley, John E. *John Dooley, Confederate Soldier: His War Journal.* Joseph T. Durkin. ed. Washington, DC: Georgetown University Press, 1945.

Douglas, Henry Kyd. *I Rode With Stonewall.* Chapel Hill: University of North Carolina Press, 1940.

Fox, William F. *Regimental Losses in the Civil War, 1861-1865.* Albany: Albany Publishing Co., 1889.

Frassanito, William A. *Antietam: The Photographic Legacy of America's Bloodiest Day.* New York: Scribner's, 1978.

Freeman, Douglas Southall. *Lee's Lieutenants.* 3 volumes. New York: Scribner's, 1942-1944.

Gallagher, Gary W. *Antietam: Essays on the 1862 Maryland Campaign.* Kent: Kent State University Press, 1989.

Johnson, Charles F. *The Long Roll.* New York, 1911.

Johnson, Robert U. and Clarence C. Buel. *Battles and Leaders of the Civil War.* 4 volumes. New York: Century, 1887-88. (Frequently reprinted.)

Livermore, Thomas L. *Numbers and Losses in the Civil War in America, 1861-1865.* Boston: Houghton Mifflin, 1902.

Longstreet, James. *From Manassas to Appomattox.* Philadelphia: Lippincott, 1896.

Murfin, James V. *The Gleam of Bayonets: The Battle of Antietam and the Maryland Campaign of 1862.* New York: Yoseloff, 1965.

Naisawald, L. Van Loan. *Grape and Cannister: The Story of the Field Artillery of the Army of the Potomac, 1861-1865.* New York: Oxford, 1960.

Palfrey, Francis W. *The Antietam and Fredericksburg.* New York: Scribner's, 1882.

Parker, Thomas H. *History of the 51st Regiment of Pennsylvania Volunteers.* Philadelphia: King & Baird, 1869.

Priest, John M. *Antietam: The Soldier's Battle.* Shippensburg, PA: White Mane, 1989.

Robertson, James. *General A.P. Hill: The Story of a Confederate Warrior.* New York: Random House, 1987.

Sauers, Richard A., ed. *The Civil War Journal of Colonel William J. Bolton, April 20, 1861–August 2, 1865.* Conshohocken, PA: Combined Publishing, 2000.

Schenck, Nathan. *Up Came Hill, The Story of the Light Division and its Commanders.* Harrisburg: Stackpole Books, 1958.

Schildt, John W. *Drums Along the Antietam.* Parsons, WV: McClain Printing Co., 1972.

Sears, Stephen W. *Landscape Turned Red: The Battle of Antietam.* New York: Ticknor & Fields, 1983.

Tucker, Phillip T. *Burnside's Bridge: The Climactic Struggle of the 2nd and 20th Georgia at Antietam Creek.* Mechanicsburg, PA: Stackpole Books, 2000.

U.S. War Department. *The War of the Rebellion: A Compilation of the Official Records of the Union and Confederate Armies.* 70 volumes. Washington, DC: Government Printing Office, 1880-1901. (Frequently reprinted.)

Wise, Jennings C. *The Long Arm of Lee: The History of the Artillery of the Army of Northern Virginia.* 1914, 1915, 1959.

Index